Red Rising and Philosophy

Popular Culture and Philosophy® Series Editor: George A. Reisch

For full details of all Popular Culture and Philosophy® books, visit www.opencourtbooks.com.

Popular Culture and Philosophy®

Red Rising and Philosophy

Break the Chains!

EDITED BY

COURTLAND LEWIS AND
KEVIN MCCAIN

OPEN COURT
Chicago

Volume 104 in the series, Popular Culture and Philosophy®, edited by George A. Reisch

To find out more about Open Court books, call toll-free 1-800-815-2280, or visit our website at www.opencourtbooks.com.

Open Court Publishing Company is a division of Carus Publishing Company, dba Cricket Media.

Red Rising and Philosophy: Break the Chains!

ISBN: 978-0-8126-9947-0

Library of Congress Control Number: 2016949364

This book is also available as an e-book.

Contents

Contents

Per Aspera ad Astra— Through the Thorns to the Stars

COURTLAND LEWIS AND KEVIN MCCAIN

What's your Color? Are you a privileged Gold, exhibiting power, strength, and wealth? Are you Pink, letting others use you for their salacious desires? Are you Blue, a good little functionary making sure other people's "toys" run smoothly? Are you Obsidian, a "thick" brute who's never considered being anything more than a tool to keep the privileged in power? Are you Red, a good little "slave," too busy working for others, preoccupied with the games and propaganda of the elite, to rise up?

Pierce Brown's world of *Red Rising* is a world of class struggles, where the rich live in luxury on the backs of the poor living in squalor. Much of society is too preoccupied with new trends and gadgets to care about the oppression, slavery, and death occurring all around them.

Sound familiar? Well, it's because it sounds a whole lot like the world of the twenty-first century, and that's why Pierce Brown's *Red Rising* series is so gripping. It slices close to home, boyo!

Bone-Peelin' Time

Whether you're a manual laborer like Darrow and the other Reds, or independently wealthy like a good Gold, *Red Rising* has an important set of lessons to which you'd be wise to pay attention. From the above-mentioned class struggles to social ordering, rape, prostitution, torture, starvation, physical enhancements, reality television, romanticized brutality, and war—oh, and uplifting things like love, friendship, overcoming adversity, and forgiveness too—*Red Rising* is like looking at a fictionalized narrative of contemporary life.

We've all wanted to do better and be better at some point in our life. Life's tough. It has a way of beating us down, and making us feel like we're stuck in a mine surrounded by pitvipers. Should we give up? *No!*

You have to take control of your life, figure out what you want, and do everything you can to achieve your dreams.

Don't know where to start? Well, neither did Darrow. At the beginning of *Red Rising* he basically gives up. He decides life isn't worth living without Eo, and he resigns himself to being executed. But from his death, he gains new life. In fact, he gains a new body, fine-tuned agility, and an enhanced brain; and with these he sets out to destroy the people who destroyed his world.

Of course, his new mission of destruction doesn't bring meaning to his life. It's not until he develops a few friendships that he actually escapes "the mines" of life.

We don't all enjoy the privilege of having our own bone-peeling carver, but the good news is that we don't need to be physically and mentally altered to change ourselves and the world. We need only the inspiration and motive to do and be greater, and a set of close friends to help us along the way; friends who will knock us down when we get too full of ourselves, and who will lift us up when we've been knocked down. This is where *Red Rising* hits closest to home.

The *Red Rising* trilogy gives us a tale of a hero who never gives up. Sure, he comes close a few times—who wouldn't after being held captive in a stone table for over a year?—but he never gives in to the temptation to quit. Darrow, Sevro, Mustang, Victra, and Ragnar show us that if we stick together and work hard enough, we can do anything to which we set our hearts and minds.

We might not all make it through, but together we can change the universe. It won't be easy, but like good philosophy, the most difficult road is often the most rewarding. The biggest battles for philosophy are self-reflection and integrity, but it's through these and other philosophically deep examinations that we grow, mature, and learn how to conquer the "Sovereigns" and "Ajas"—both within ourselves and in the world—who are out to destroy us.

Our Iron Rain

Red Rising and Philosophy has gathered together some of the most razor-sharp Howlers, Helldivers, and Peerless Scarred this side of Mars. We're all different Colors from different Houses, but we don't give a bloodydamn about those sorts of things. All we care about is using logic and clear reasoning to bring down the Society of ignorance that's keeping us mentally enslaved.

Could our love of physical and mental enhancements cause humanity's extinction? Do we doom humanity by trying to all be the same? Can you love someone, while at the same time wanting them destroyed? How should society be structured, and is equality always the best principle on which to organize it? What is evil, and how does it exist in contemporary life? Should you love, forgive, or seek revenge against those who you hate? Are you the same person, even after you change every physical aspect of your body? If you're no longer the same person, are you still required to keep promises you made to yourself or your loved ones? What sort of limits should we put on weapons? Can an oppressive society be beautiful? Oh, and what's the meaning of life?

See, we're not afraid of any question! Just like Pierce Brown, we pull no punches, because philosophy works best in an environment with open and honest dialogue—it's like the Institute without all of the rape, murder, and cannibalism. *Red Rising and Philosophy* isn't for the timid or the faint at heart. It's not the Passage, since no one will die from reading it, but it could change your life.

You might even start your own Rising, but only if you're willing to open your mind to the lessons within. On your journey, you might gain some insights and wisdom that'll help you do more than merely survive in this world. You might just learn how to flourish, no matter who you are or where you find yourself in this life.

Thinkers of the world, . . . Unite!

Let's dance forbidden dances and sing Eo's forbidden song.

I

Conundrums
for the
Quality Control
Board

1
When Evolution Strikes Back

TIM JONES

That you're able to read and understand the *Red Rising* trilogy is nothing short of a miracle.

Before you wonder what this bloodydamn Violet is daring to insinuate about your intelligence, calm down, that's not what I'm talking about. I'm actually referring to the many ways in which the human mind and body has had to adapt to make the act of reading possible.

First of all, there's language itself. Our brains have developed to recognize that certain sounds stand-in for certain objects or concepts, and that certain physical shapes, when written down on paper, act as further visual stand-ins for these sounds. These shapes couldn't fulfill this function if you weren't able to actually see them—we might take the gift of sight for granted, but for the majority of the 3.8 billion years in which there's been life on Earth, none of the creatures around had anything that we'd call an eye.

And being able to hold the book in front of you and turn the pages is pretty handy too. Opposable thumbs are useful here and partially explain why your cat or dog isn't easily able to share *Red Rising and Philosophy* with you when you're done. Just a few reasons, then, why you're able to enjoy Pierce Brown's trilogy, while the earliest life-forms who crawled out of the sea wouldn't have been. Must've gorydamn sucked to be them.

The valuable changes between these first creatures and ourselves come down to evolution. Evolution is the process by which organisms change over millions of years in ways that are beneficial to their species's long-term survival, giving successive generations advantages that previous generations did not have. The end result is that each species that doesn't become extinct should eventually reach its perfected form, gradually becoming better and better suited to thriving in its home environment. Sometimes the changes can even be dramatic enough for the creation of a new species altogether, which will be better suited to its environment than the species it evolved from!

Bloodydamn Process

This process doesn't always run without a hitch. An environmental catastrophe might come along and derail it by plunging an entire ecosystem into an unpredicted chaos, threatening fitter and less fit organisms alike. And as environments change over time, so too will the qualities necessary to be the best-suited for survival there. But whatever happens, evolution will always be hard at work in the background playing catch-up, helping whichever creatures are there become better and better suited to thrive in whatever environmental conditions are currently enduring.

No wonder that Charles Darwin's ground-breaking book on the subject, *On the Origin of Species* (1859), makes evolution sound absolutely beautiful. He even characterizes the Nature who guides evolution as a female hero figure with her own direct agency, which she puts towards furthering her wonderful plans for improving life as much as it can possibly be improved. I think he used this slightly odd literary device as a way of engaging with the respect for God that would've been ingrained into much of his nineteenth-century readership. If you're trying to get people to listen to ideas they're gonna find really hard to get their heads around, you can help your cause by doing your best to make those ideas look like something they're already familiar with. Forgive me for repeating his trick throughout this chapter.

But Darwin's actually a little too enamored of Nature's project not to gloss over the dark side of the evolutionary story—that the perfection of each species is achieved through its weakest and less well-adapted members losing in the struggle for life to the strongest, so that only they get to pass on their winning characteristics to the next generation. Darwin's personified version of Nature may be less of a hero and more of an anti-hero with some pretty psychotic tendencies that she might want to get checked out, achieving her goals through the extermination of millions of beings who don't fit her criteria.

Mass murderers like Hitler and Stalin were both able to give their appalling acts of violence a noble sheen through their belief that they were only helping Nature achieve her wonderful plan. They tried accelerating the process of perfection-seeking by killing off races or classes that history would inevitably cast away as defunct anyway, so they might as well be disposed of sooner rather than later.

The ruling Golds follow these historical monsters by also justifying some pretty terrible things. They shared Darwin's belief that Nature's work is beautiful, and concluded that it's therefore great to help her along, as we can see from just the first page of *Red Rising*. The Golds see themselves as this perfected end-point of human evolution, which is a position that entitles them to subjugate the lesser classes. And we soon learn that the purpose of the Passage and the Institute is to provide the right sort of environment to see the weaker Golds killed in order to make sure that only the very best of the Gold gene-pool is allowed to reach maturity. Just as Darrow says, in the moment that he kills Julian he becomes "Darwin's scythe," separating the Gold wheat from the Gold chaff so that the former can prosper.

So evolution has been way more beneficial to the Golds than it has been to you, not just letting them read books like the one you're holding now, but also giving them the justification to subjugate all those beneath them on the Color pyramid, while ensuring too that their own Color remains untainted by imperfection.

Or maybe it hasn't after all. Because the Golds have fatally misunderstood a key part of Darwin's argument regarding how evolution works. By the end of *Morning Star*, it looks like Nature was never on their side at all. While they think they've been helping her along and reaping the benefits, they've actually just been making it easier for her to destroy their project through their manipulations of the lower Colors hand-crafting the means by which their Hierarchy will be pulled apart.

Nature Versus Nurture

To understand how exactly the Golds have fatally misunderstood evolution and made themselves its victims rather than its champions, we can go back to Darwin himself and look at the distinctions he draws between *natural* evolution and the *man-made* alternative Golds work upon the classes that eventually overthrow them.

It's a common misconception that Darwin was the Yellow who first discovered evolution. The idea that individual species change over time is basically already there in Ancient Greek accounts of animal forms emerging from primordial slime. And in the decades more immediately before Darwin, there's Jean-Baptiste Lamarck's *Philosophie Zoologique* (1809) and Robert Chambers's *The Vestiges of Creation* (1844), both of which observe that plant and animal species haven't remained entirely static through the ages. What helped the idea gain currency in the nineteenth-century was the monumental revelation that the world wasn't only six thousand years old, as the Bible indicates, but countless hundreds of million years instead. I wonder if it's even possible to comprehend today how dramatic a shift this was—an astronomically bigger shattering of people's perceived place in the universe than even the lowReds' realization that Mars has already been perfectly terraformed for centuries.

How did this revelation help? Well, it was easy to strike down previous advocates of evolution with facts like images of animals on the tombs of the Pharaohs not looking any different from their contemporary cats and dogs—surely you can see from this that the very idea of animals evolving over time is palpable nonsense! But this counter-argument relies on the temporal gap between Egyptian times and the present day being a pretty large slice of all the time that has *ever* passed. When it's revealed that these two thousand years are only the teeniest, tiniest fraction of world history, then suddenly there's bags of room for the species around us to have been very different when the world began and to have changed and adapted over millennia.

So in the nineteenth century there's a new understanding of the true span of world time that makes evolution just a little more palatable. It's not a new idea, but more people are ready to talk about it, and more people are ready to listen, even if the majority were still deeply offended by what they heard. And what Darwin adds to the debate is Natural Selection, as the tool by which evolution actually operates. (This might be another reason why he keeps referring to "Nature" as though she's an actual person—the phrase "Natural Selection" kind of necessitates the presence of someone or something *doing* the actual selecting . . .)

If you take a look at Darwin's *On the Origin of Species*, you'll quickly get his point that life is gorydamn hard. A struggle for existence. Each species competes not only with all of the other species around it for the limited resources that are needed to survive, but also with its own fellow members. I don't know what the pitvipers that infest the tunnels under Mars are meant to live on (perhaps the bodies of those unlucky Reds who get crushed in rock falls), but whatever this food source is, it's inevitably finite in quantity, and so not all of the pitvipers are going to be able to get enough of it to live on. The result is a competition for this finite resource between each individual pitviper. Some will get to chow down on what's available, while others will miss out.

Evolution through Natural Selection is the result of this competition. Why exactly do some pitvipers get to eat, while others don't? I've been unable to get close enough for these points to be more than speculative, but they might have more athletic bodies, so that they can more quickly slither to the fallen Red; or they might have sharper teeth, to more effectively scare away any other pitvipers who want to steal the buffet. These pitvipers with more athletic bodies and sharper teeth will get to live on to the point where they experience the joy of having pitviper babies, while the others do not. These pitviper babies will inherit the characteristics of their successful parents, meaning that successive generations of pitviper babies will have more athletic bodies and sharper teeth than those that came before. And so, thanks to Natural Selection, pitvipers will, over the millennia, become increasingly great at doing all the stuff that pitvipers need to do if they're to thrive under Mars. These are natural laws that function entirely under their own steam, without any human interference or guidance necessary. Life's pretty miraculous like that.

But this isn't the only means by which creatures can evolve. *On the Origin of Species* contrasts evolution as performed by Natural Selection with evolution as performed by human intervention. Every time we breed something like a sheep or a dog to accentuate one characteristic over others in its offspring, we're basically doing the same work as Nature in forcing that species to change along particular lines. So farm animals will end up with more and more meat, while border collies will end up with an increased instinct for herding.

Darwin is pretty judgemental about how man-made variations in a species stack up against Nature's own craftwork, particularly when he considers the motivations behind them. We force animals to develop for entirely selfish reasons, serving our interests rather than theirs, while evolution guided by Nature helps each species perfect its own potential. He makes it sound like Nature would be pretty angry about humans forcing species to develop in such a self-serving way, while her own developments are ones of visionary grandeur.

It's ironically fitting, then, that Nature should choose the man-made variations that the Golds have made upon the lowReds to be her tool for bringing the entire Color hierarchy crashing to the ground. It's her perfect revenge upon the Golds for citing her rules as justification for placing the rest of humankind in their thrall, while only forcing evolution along their own limiting lines in the process.

The Golds Done Messed Up

The Golds are arrogant enough to interfere with evolution in two ways. Their own rituals involving the Institute and the Passage might sound fairly like Natural Selection at work, since once the young Golds end up in the environment in question, they're left pretty much entirely to their own devices until the strongest or the craftiest wins out. But this is still a process that's more man-made than Natural.

Sure, the Golds are working to improve their own stock here, rather than doing what a farmer or a dog-trainer would do by improving another species for his or her own benefit. But the Institute isn't exactly a natural habitat that the Golds would inevitably find themselves in; it's a man-made arena with parameters and rules artificially set by the elite, with people forced into its space by its creators, rather than naturally inhabiting it. At best, then, it's a hijacking of Natural Selection that forces it to function according to humankind's own vision and to humankind's own sense of what would make us great.

If Nature were able to perfect the Golds according to her own design, she might never place them in such an environment. She might disagree that the characteristics needed to live through it are actually the best for the Golds' long-term survival, or, for that matter, that having people like the Golds in charge is best for humanity as a whole. There's no telling which characteristics or qualities she'd choose to accentuate, instead of the physical strength and mental sneakiness that the Golds who usually win the Institute likely possess.

Darwin's alternative phrase for Natural Selection, "survival of the fittest," has often been misinterpreted to mean *physically* fittest, or strongest—the best able to win in a barfight at a dive like Luna's Lost Wee Den. If we understand 'fittest' as also meaning, in a less specific sense, 'best suited', then you may see instead that you can be best suited to surviving in places that aren't like the Institute through a whole range of other characteristics, beyond brute force.

The most suited to survival in a kinder environment might actually be the people most willing to co-operate rather than compete, or refuse to fight rather than kill each other. The Jackal survived the Institute, but he ended up learning that the best way to get what you want is to load an entire planetoid up with nuclear bombs and detonate them one at a time whenever someone says "no." As I said at the start, Nature clearly wanted you to evolve to be able to read *Red Rising*, but I doubt she'd be as happy about a man like the Jackal rising to the top of the pyramid. It's less likely to lead towards humankind's perfection than it is to its destruction!

So the Golds' use of the Institute is one way that they interfere with Nature's approach towards evolution—and one that clearly isn't likely to lead to a happily perfected class of Golds like they think it is. The second way involves their manipulation of the rest of humanity via the strict Color pyramid. And just like the first, Nature ensures that this too serves only to screw them over.

Mickey the Carver versus Life as a Red

While the Golds work to improve their own stock via the misguided rite of the Institute, they've also been working on the rest of humankind much like we work on our farm animals or pets, cultivating certain characteristics in them that make them better suited to serving the Golds' own interests.

Pinks are conditioned to please through the application and removal of physical pain. The Pinks that don't learn this lesson pretty quick probably won't survive in their vocation long enough to get the opportunity to have children, while the ones that do will, so successive generations of Pink will take to the task of pleasing their masters ever more readily and with less forced conditioning required each time. We see during the chat between Augustus, Pliny, and Darrow near the start of *Golden Son* that they've worked similarly on the

Reds, deliberately designing Red society to be patriarchal so that the necessary qualities for them to be up to their "physically strenuous, gruelling" work are accentuated over any characteristics that would be irrelevant for such a life.

Darrow achieves a lot during his stints as a counterfeit Gold and an unmasked Son of Ares. Conquering Olympus at the Institute, an Iron Rain against Mars, and the capture of the Sword Armada, to name just a few of the barely conceivable successes that make his campaign against the Color hierarchy ultimately win out. And while Darrow gives a lot of credit for his victories to the abilities given to him by Mickey the Carver, if we track the things he actually finds useful, they're equally thanks to the carvings that the Golds themselves have made to all the lowReds destined to toil under Mars's surface.

When Darrow kills Julian in the Passage, he doesn't attribute his victory to any skills granted by his conversion from Red to Gold, but to the strength of his "Helldiver knuckles"—attributes picked up during his work down in the mines. The crazy momentum with which he leaps from plan to plan across all three stories is likewise the result of his Father teaching him that "a Helldiver can never stop" for fear of the drill jamming, or the fuel burning out, or the vital helium-3 quota getting missed. His courage before the Iron Rain as his fleet gathers around Phobos is due to a life where death from a rock fall or explosion might come at any time. The dexterity he needed there as a miner is what makes him able to pull himself out from the mud after the EMP detonation by the walls of the Martian city Agea.

Perhaps the greatest example I could possibly give you of this trend is his genius plan for the rebels to clawDrill their way through Roque's boarding parties on their passage through space between the *Pax* and the Sword Amada's *Colossus*. Then again, perhaps Darrow would've failed at stopping additional nuclear bombs detonating during the final confrontation on Luna, if it weren't for his miner's instinct to rip out the Jackal's tongue just like he would a pitviper, stopping him from giving the command for all-out destruction.

So Mickey's work on Darrow would never have been enough all on its own. It's almost secondary to all of the traits that Darrow inherited through the Golds' deliberate cultivation of the lowReds. While the Golds imagined they constructed a perfect slave class, instead they unwittingly created the tools of their own Hierarchy's undoing.

Survival of the Fittest

All of the time that the Golds imagined themselves as the very end-point of human evolution, Nature was actually waiting for the perfect moment to begin her own project of making their Hierarchy extinct. It's especially fitting that the main tool she uses is one of their own making. The evolutionary processes that they felt in perfect control of instead become the architects of their doom. Don't get Nature pissed, or she'll gorywell mess you up.

I don't think it's even just spite or jealousy about her processes being appropriated that's got her so pissed in the first place. According to Darwin, evolution working through Natural Selection is Nature's way of leading all species towards perfection. And Quicksilver gives us in *Morning Star* an explanation for how exactly the Golds might have been obstructing Nature's goal, and why removing their hierarchy is necessary for her if she's to get her work back on track.

A regime like the Golds', Quicksilver tells us, keeps humanity entirely static and its development stifled. Without individuals being able freely to compete for the job or vocation of their choosing, to be promoted within according to their ability and results (rather than set by their Color at birth), humanity will never advance as a species as much as we could if every position in society were open to the person with the strongest talent or will. With the Hierarchy in place, stopping this nurturing of individual potential in all but the most privileged, humanity might never extend beyond the solar system to explore the billions of planets throughout the expanse of deep space. The Golds are then not the apex of humanity, but its brake. The fittest only at keeping us from achieving our true potential.

You may or may not agree with Quicksilver's passionate advocacy of capitalism as the perfect solution to the stifling nature of the Color hierarchy. You might think that he's suffering from a classic case of the grass being greener (or golder) on the other side, and that by growing up in a capitalist society ourselves we can see that capitalism would only introduce an alternative series of privileges and marginalizations, based around the money you're born into, rather than the Color. The new system might end up looking remarkably like the old and feature pretty much the same limiting effect on humanity reaching its potential. Or you might be totally on his side.

"Which system is most likely to lead us to our full potential?" is a difficult question! But then again, given what happens to the Golds when Nature deems that the best system is definitely not the one that *they*'ve created, perhaps it's not one for us to worry about answering.

Perhaps we should just leave it to Nature to work out what's best for us and let her bring it into being by her own means and in her own time, without us looking to hurry her along.

2
Not So Human After All?

BRENDAN SHEA

In the future described in the *Red Rising* novels, many Golds believe they *deserve* to rule over the other Colors. They believe this, at least in part, because of the *biological* differences introduced by the use of genetic engineering. Gold women and men are on average faster, stronger, longer-lived, and (in their view) more "intelligent" than the other Colors.

It's with this in mind that Adrius "The Jackal" suggests that Reds really do form a different species (*Homo flameus*) from either the *Homo sapiens* from which both Golds and Reds descend or the Golds themselves that dominate all Colors. Later, in *Morning Star*, he claims that Darrow is "not even evolved enough to have a Color . . . Just a *Homo sapiens* playing in the realm of the gods." Again, the suggestion is that individual Colors represent different species, with the Golds representing the "highest" species.

The stories suggest that the Jackal's view about the relationship between the Colors might be, at least to some extent, an idiosyncratic one, reflective of his own warped view of reality. Darrow, for one, argues that the Jackal is "just a man." Moreover, even powerful highColors such as Octavia au Lune and Quicksilver talk about the human "species" in ways that suggest they see it as a single community, instead of a set of different species (even if Octavia thinks that Golds are uniquely qualified to lead the community). However, none of these people actually offer an *argument* against the Jackal's claims concerning the biological relationships between the various Colors.

It's easy enough to show that the Golds are not literally gods. However, this doesn't get to the heart of the Jackal's claim that the Golds really are different from the other Colors, and that these differences provide a justification for the Golds' treatment of them. In this respect, it seems that the Jackal's claim is merely an exaggerated version of what many Golds already accept. Moreover, it has clear parallels with the way that high-status groups in our own world have often tried to "justify" their treatment of other "lesser" groups.

Aristotle's Essentialism Rising

In our day-to-day to lives, we frequently distinguish between species of animals by looking for some "unique" characteristic that distinguishes them from otherwise similar species. Squirrels, for example, have bushy tales while chipmunks don't. American robins have red breasts while blackbirds are black. Humans have the ability to speak languages that chimpanzees can't.

In the future described by *Red Rising*, it seems as though an average adult could probably do the same with regards to their own various Colors, given their distinctive appearances and unique physical characteristics. The size and color of an Obsidian, for example, makes it unlikely that she will be confused for a Red or Pink.

Aristotle, the so-called "father of biology," based his account of species on just this sort of idea. In particular, he proposed that an organism's biological species was fixed by its having—or failing to have—the properties *essential* to that species, which served to differentiate that species from other species in the same genus. Aristotle defined humans, for example, as the "rational animal," since he thought it was our human capacity to *reason* (which included the use of language) that served to distinguish us from the larger group of animals.

Aristotle's account holds that the borders between species are both clear-cut and immutable, which fits well with the later idea that each had been created by the separate act of an all-powerful God for a specific purpose. It also suggested a theory of what it means to be a *good* or *successful* human (one ought to be as rational as possible), and to the relationship between humans and other species (animals, for example, were meant to be used by humans). It also seems to fit well with the Jackal's claim that the Colors represent different species.

The Colors were specifically designed by genetic engineering to fulfill distinctive tasks: Reds to mine, Pinks for pleasure, Silver to deal with money, Golds to rule, and so on. The Jackal would be especially pleased to learn that Aristotle himself proposed that some humans were "natural slaves," who could fulfill their human potential only by allowing themselves to be governed by the reason of *someone else*.

Happily, Aristotle's claims about natural slaves, and about the essential nature of species, find little support in post-Darwinian biology. As it turns out, because of genetic variation, it's frequently impossible to find any property (or group of properties) that perfectly distinguishes one species from another. Not every human is more intelligent than every chimp, for example, just as not every Red is shorter than every Gold. Moreover, the last 150 years of biological research shows that species themselves change and evolve over time, with some species going extinct, and others slowly emerging from other species. The mere fact that Golds were originally "designed" to rule and Reds "designed" to mine doesn't provide any reason for thinking that these roles can't change, or that society might not be better off if Reds were given an equal voice in government. Biology, it turns out, is not destiny.

Species as Individuals

In contrast to Aristotle's view that species are abstract *types* or *categories* of organisms, many contemporary biologists and philosophers of biology tend to think of species as *individuals,* in somewhat the same way that organisms are individuals. So, just as many individual cells make up an individual human body, many individual humans make up the species *Homo sapiens.* This view, unlike Aristotle's, doesn't presuppose that there's any characteristic that serves to differentiate the members of the species from all others. Species are simply groups of related organisms (or "lineages") that live (or lived) in particular times and places.

Of course, claiming that species are lineages doesn't actually answer the question: "Where does one species end and another begin?" It doesn't, for example, tell us whether Reds and Golds are separate species, or whether either (or both) of these are the same species as current-day *Homo sapiens.*

As it turns out, contemporary biologists and philosophers have proposed many different answers to this question. Let's take a look at three popular species concepts: one based on interbreeding, one based on shared ancestry, and a final one based on adaptations to the surrounding environment. In the real world, new species usually emerge slowly, perhaps over millions of years. In the *Red Rising* universe, by contrast, the widespread use of genetic engineering has made things very different, as evidenced by the "Carved" creatures they can create.

The most widely known species concept is probably Ernst Mayr's Biological Species Concept, which holds that species are groups of organisms that are capable of interbreeding with each other, but which are reproductively isolated from other such groups. According to this view, for example, horses and pigs are separate species, since they are completely incapable of breeding with each other. However, it turns out that horses and donkeys are *also* separate species, since their hybrid offspring (such as mules) are themselves sterile.

When applied to the *Red Rising* universe, this view suggests that Golds and Reds really might form separate species, just as Adrius claims. The results of past genetic engineering have left Gold-Red pairs incapable of reproducing "naturally," as evidenced by the significant efforts that Sevro's parents took in order to conceive him. Moreover, these formidable physical barriers to reproduction are sup-plemented by additional social and environmental ones, not the least of which is their Society's violent reactions to "hy-brids" and their parents. These sorts of barriers preventing gene flow between Golds and Reds all have analogues in the natural world, where species are isolated from one another by geography and mating rituals, and not just by their re-productive physiology.

For all its simplicity, however, the Biological Species Con-cept has a number of drawbacks.

First, as Sevro's example makes apparent, the barriers preventing one group of organisms from interbreeding with another are often less than perfect. Because of this, we have to make decisions about just how much isolation is "good enough" to count as a new species. It seems likely that Dar-row and Adrius may disagree on how this applies to the dif-ferences between the Colors.

Second, this concept doesn't apply *at all* to beings that don't reproduce sexually. In our world, these organisms (which form the majority of all life) consist primarily of bac-teria, but in the world of *Red Rising*, things are considerably different. It's suggested, for example, that Pinks may be per-manently sterile. If this is the case, then they may well re-produce by asexual means (perhaps they are clones grown in vats, or implanted in surrogate mothers?). If this were the case, Mayr's Biological Species Concept would hold that Pinks don't belong to *any* species, even if all of the other Col-ors do, as Adrius claims. This result is, to put it mildly, a bit disconcerting.

Golden Alternatives to the Biological Species Concept

The Phylogenetic Species Concept represents a prominent alternative to the Biological Species Concept. According to this concept, biological groupings (including species, but also genus, family, and so on) should include all and only those organisms descending from a common ancestor. In the context of *Red Rising*, this concept might give a variety of answers to the species question, depending on *which* ancestor you start from. For example, Golds and Reds both descend from an ancient human common ancestor, and so we might plausibly count all three groups (Gold, Reds, "old" humans) as being members of the species *Homo sapiens.*

However, given his dedication to highlighting differences between the Colors, the Jackal might well choose to focus on more recent ancestors, who were themselves Golds and Reds. By this definition, Golds and Reds would again be separate species. Unlike the Biological Species Concept, the Phylogenetic Species Concept can also account for asexual species, so Pinks (and bacteria) would no longer be a "problem" case for Adrius.

Just as with the Biological Species Concept, however, the Phylogenetic Species Concept runs into problems. First, it has a problem in dealing with splinter groups that break off from a larger group, and form new species. Let's suppose that the Jackal is right, and that Golds really are a different species than the other colors. However, let's complicate things a bit, and pretend that Silvers, at some point, broke off from the early Golds. So, perhaps the early Golds decided to design a new Color, and (as a starting point) used the DNA from one or more Golds. According to the Phylogenetic Species Concept, this leaves us with a dilemma regarding the relation of the Golds living after the Gold-Silver split with those living before it.

If Adrius wants to claim that he (and other current Golds) are the *same species* as the old, pre-split Golds, the Phylogenetic Species Concept will force him to admit that the Silvers are *not* a different species, since both groups descend from the same common ancestor (a pre-split Gold). By contrast, if Adrius wants to claim that current Golds and current Silvers really are different species, then he *also* has to admit that the current Golds are a different species than the pre-split Golds. The one thing the Phylogenetic Species Concept (not to mention consistent reasoning) will absolutely not allow is for Adrius to claim that he is both: 1. the same species as the old Golds, and 2. a different species from modern Silvers. Confusing, right?

This same problem appears in a different way when we consider the (presumably widespread) genetic engineering of the *Red Rising* Society, and the way this allows genetic information to flow back and forth between the Colors. Suppose, for instance, scientists discover that certain genes are linked to increased strength in a certain tribe of Obsidians. They might (reasonably) use this information to alter Golds to make *them* (and their offspring) stronger. As a consequence, the new, stronger generation of Golds can trace their genetic descent not just from their Gold parents, but also (indirectly) from the Obsidians and *their* ancestors. Now, we're left with a puzzle: "Does this prove that Obsidians and Golds are the same species, after all?" We might be tempted to say "yes," until we remember that this sort of horizontal gene transfer need not involve a closely related group, but could've come from a far different sort of organism, such an insect or a fish. So, it seems like the Phylogenetic Species Concept cannot definitively answer our question after all.

A third concept of species, the Ecological Species Concept, identifies species with those lineages adapted to specific environmental niches. Reds, for instance, are adapted to working in cramped mines, while Blues are "made" to live in spaceships. Moreover, the differing demands of these environments play a key role in explaining *why* the groups stay separate. So, for example, it seems like the genetic makeup of each Color was originally *designed* for optimal performance in its respective niche, and that subsequent evolution has, if anything, pushed the Colors further and further apart, as subsequent generations of Blues have genomes rendering them ever more suitable for spaceflight, while Reds' genomes make them better and better miners. Unlike the Biological or Phylogenetic species concepts, this makes no assumptions about Reds' and Blues' capacities to interbreed with one another, nor about precise relationships among their ancestors. According to this theory, again, it seems as if the Jackal may have won the day.

Just as was the case with the first two species concepts, however, there are reasons to be skeptical of the Jackal's claim, as the Ecological Species Concept can quickly lead to strange conclusions. Not all Reds, for instance, live on Mars: some might live on Luna, or on the moons of Jupiter. Moreover, while their niche in these places may still involve mining, this may occur under far different conditions: the gravity may be weaker, the atmosphere different, and so on, all of which could easily lead to genetic differences in future generations (especially given the aggressive applications of genetic engineering techniques). However, it would be very strange to think of these Reds as a different species from Mars Red, especially if they shared a common descent with other Reds, and are capable of interbreeding. A much more radical change in the Reds' niche is suggested by Darrow's and Mustang's success, which will free future Reds to do much more than they ever have. When we take account of all of this, we are again pushed toward the idea that "they are all just humans, after all." Again, though, it seems that Ecological Species Concept isn't capable of deciding one way or other.

Why Should We Care?

In the end, then, it seems as if our concepts of species aren't really designed to answer the question "Are the various Colors really different species?"—or at least can't do so without much more data. They neither provide definite support for the Jackal's claims, nor provide an easy method for refuting him.

Darwin himself argued that this sort of phenomenon was much more widespread than people recognized. Among other things, he suggested that there was often no clear line between what counted as a *species* and what counted as a *variety* within a species, and that nature simply didn't match up with humanity's demands that the living world be divided neatly into discrete species. This wasn't merely a problem of our ignorance, but of the way the world is. If Darwin is right, it simply might be that the argument between Adrius and

Darrow has no single, objectively correct answer, in part because our normal ways of thinking about what species are don't work well when applied to scenarios described in *Red Rising*.

So, what does this mean for the society of *Red Rising*, and for us?

First, it's important to recognize the *irrelevance* of the biological distinctions being debated here to the sorts of moral and political questions that lie at the heart of the Jackal's and Darrow's disagreements. Even if the Golds are a different species, for example, this doesn't mean that they have justification for treating the Colors in the way they do. This would be the case even if Adrius were *correct* in thinking that the Golds are (on average) stronger and smarter than the other Colors.

The philosopher Peter Singer, among others, has forcefully argued that it's a mistake to think that the moral *equality* between individuals depends on their being equally intelligent or physically capable. Instead, moral equality derives from the fact that other people—regardless of their gender, race, disability status, cognitive ability, or anything else—have interests, just the same as we do. The reason it's wrong for the Golds to enslave Reds is because Reds, just like Golds, want something better from their lives.

A second related point concerns the importance of things *besides* biology in creating and maintaining distinctions between the Colors. Being born a Gold, for instance, provides you with much different (and much more advantageous) education and upbringing than being born a Red. Gold children are brought up learning they're "meant" to rule, while Red children are taught they are "meant" to be miners.

These sorts of differences are present in almost every aspect of their lives—the jobs they work, the way they raise their children, the religions and stories they're exposed to, and so on. These non-biological differences are, without a doubt, at the heart of the reason Adrius finds his proposed system of biological classification so attractive: he just *knows* that Golds are meant to rule, and he's determined to find

23

biological differences that make the distinctions he's already committed to making. It shouldn't be too surprising that, when he goes looking for some sort of biological differences between Colors, he can (sort of) find them. However, it's crucially important to keep in mind that Adrius's proposed classification wasn't arrived at by a disinterested consideration of the biological evidence, and that it certainly doesn't support his belief that Golds are superior to the other Colors. This holds lessons for the real world: we ought to be especially skeptical when we "discover" that biology provides support for our pre-existing biases.

The final point to note is that, in the end, we should recognize that the "correct" way to make biological distinctions will frequently depend on what we're trying to do. Biologists, for example, often use the different concepts of species described here to measure the "biodiversity" of an environment, so that this research can guide efforts to maintain or protect this diversity. Given this sort of goal, the fact that there's "no single right answer" to the question "How many species are there?" need not pose any difficultly. Each of the three species concepts provides us with valuable information about the diversity of life, all of which might be relevant to us.

In the case of *Red Rising*, the challenge facing Mustang and Darrow at the end of the books is a very different one: how can they can help create a society that treats *all* of its citizens (regardless of their Color) fairly and equitably? Biological research may well have a role to play in helping to bring this about; however, it can do so effectively only if accompanied by the wisdom to interpret its findings in ways that allow them to overcome the particular barriers they encounter.

3
Hero or Villain?

Kevin McCain

Surely we can tell the difference between a hero and a villain. For example, obviously Darrow, the Reaper of Mars, is a hero of *Red Rising*. Just as obvious is the fact that Nero au Augustus is a villain—the slagging bastard hanged Eo for singing a song!

But, when we stop and really think about it maybe things aren't quite so clear. Recall, this conversation between Mustang and Darrow (*Golden Son*, p. 291):

> **MUSTANG:** You can still cut me away like *that*. You care and then you don't. Maybe that's why he likes you so much.
>
> **DARROW:** He?
>
> **MUSTANG:** My father.
>
> **DARROW:** He doesn't like me.
>
> **MUSTANG:** How could he not? *You are him.*

You might be thinking that Mustang is just being bloody-damn foolish here. There's no way that Darrow is like her father, Nero au Augustus! Admittedly, when Darrow insists that he's not like Augustus, Mustang relents. She says, "I know . . . That's not fair to you." However, are they really so different? What is it that makes one a hero and the other a villain? Let's explore the issue here and see what we can learn from it, prime?

Mirror Images?

Despite the fact that we feel bloodydamn sure that Darrow is a hero and Nero is a villain, it's slagging hard to deny that they have a lot of things in common! Consider the facts, my goodman or goodwoman.

Darrow and Nero share many features. On the positive side, they both have lofty, noble goals. Darrow is determined to bring down the corrupt Society and usher in a new order that better realizes Eo's dream of a universe where all Colors are free. No doubt about it, that's a noble goal.

As much as it may pain us to admit, it seems that Nero au Augustus is equally consumed with a noble goal. He refuses to let the human race end. As he says, "I would have us continue forever . . . I would make man the immutable fixture of the universe" (*Golden Son*, p. 430). We might quibble over whether it's truly noble to desire that any species (even our own) continues on beyond the death of our sun, but at least on its face this seems like a noble goal. Slag, even Darrow admits that Nero is pursuing a noble goal. After all, when he learns of Nero's aspirations Darrow grudgingly thinks to himself that Nero "is a noble man doing what he thinks is best for humanity. Damn him" (*Golden Son*, p. 432).

Not only are Darrow and Nero alike in sharing noble goals, they have many admirable qualities in common too. For instance, both men are extremely intelligent. They are both determined to achieve their goals. They are willing to make sacrifices. They're brave. And so on. Hence, it seems that Darrow and Nero are very similar when it comes to possessing many praiseworthy qualities. So, they're both heroes? No, there's a turd in the swillbowl here.

Darrow and Nero have noble goals, and they share many noble qualities. Nonetheless, there are many darker traits that both share as well. They are both killers. All Peerless Scarred have killed in the Passage. Since the Passage is a kill or be killed situation, we might say that neither Darrow nor Nero had a choice but to kill in that circumstance though. Setting aside the Passage, both men have killed numerous people. Darrow and Nero have both killed people themselves, and they've both ordered others to kill people. Even if they had no choice when it came to some of these killings, not all of them were instances of self-defense.

Although killing and ordering deaths are the worst of their common qualities, there are several other ignoble traits that Darrow and Nero share. Both of these men are manipulative, and they both lie when it suits their needs. As we noted above, both are willing to make sacrifices, which in some cases is an admirable quality. Unfortunately, they're both willing to make sacrifices of other people—when they sacrifice other people's lives to further their own ends being willing to make sacrifices is not something to be admired anymore.

Finally, both are prideful to a fault. Being proud seems like a good thing, but only up to a point. Too much pride is a moral failing, and Darrow and Nero share this flaw. Fortunately for Darrow he learns from the mistakes caused by his hubris. In *Morning Star* we find Darrow a much humbler man; he is no longer overly proud. Nero never learns to temper his pride. So, perhaps they are different in this way, but that's not much.

Darrow and Nero are very similar in a number of ways. It is also clear that both are very far from perfect. Nevertheless, we're still inclined to judge them differently. We say that Darrow is a hero and Nero isn't. We cheer Darrow on and hope that Nero fails. Why? What makes the one a hero and the other a villain?

The Ends Justify the Means?

Let's start with consequentialism. Very roughly put, this is the moral theory that says the ends justify the means. According to consequentialist moral theories, whether an action is right or wrong, good or bad is solely a matter of the consequences of the action. As long as the good consequences outweigh the bad, the act is right.

This is exactly the sort of thinking that Harmony employs when she sends Evey on a suicide mission without Evey even knowing it. When Darrow questions her about sacrificing Evey, Harmony responds, "I'd sacrifice any of us to kill a Peerless Scarred" (*Golden Son*, p. 75). She thinks that as long as the end result is good enough it can justify whatever means are necessary.

This isn't just the thinking of Harmony though; it's the heart of one of the better-known theories of morality: utilitarianism. There are various forms that utilitarianism can take, but they all share a commitment to consequentialism. They all say that the only factor that matters when it comes to whether an action is good or bad to perform is the utility (goods) that is ultimately produced by the action.

Classical utilitarians such as Jeremy Bentham and John Stuart Mill hold that utility is simply a matter of happiness (understood in terms of pleasure and the absence of pain). According to this kind of thinking, whether Harmony was right to sacrifice Evey to kill the Jackal (the target of Harmony's attack) depends upon the overall happiness produced as a result of her action. If the action produces the best balance of happiness for everyone affected (when everyone's happiness is taken collectively), then it's right. If not, then it's wrong.

You might find this sort of ends-justify-the-means thinking implausible, my goodman or goodwoman. You wouldn't be alone in thinking this. Yet, our goal here isn't to determine whether utilitarianism, or any other form of consequentialism, is correct. Instead, we're simply interested in determining whether some form of consequentialism can give us grounds to think that Darrow is a hero and Nero isn't. Apparently, it can't.

Both Darrow and Nero appeal to consequentialist reasoning in justifying some of the ways in which they attempt to reach their goals. When Darrow has to secure the support of Romulus au Raa, Archgovernor of Io, he justifies his sacrifice of dockworkers and many others on the grounds that it's necessary for him to win his war against the Society in the core of the solar system. Darrow thinks to himself "I swallow the guilt of leaving hundreds of millions in slavery and personally signing the death warrants of thousands of Sons of Ares to Romulus's police" (*Morning Star*, p. 388).

Darrow is relying on consequentialism to justify his actions—the ends (bringing down the Sovereign and the Society in the core) justify the means (leaving hundreds of millions in slavery and allowing Romulus to kill thousands of Sons in the outer reaches of the solar system).

Nero expresses similar reasoning when Darrow questions him about how far he'll go to realize his goal of preserving humanity. Darrow accuses Nero, "You bomb innocent civilians, who haven't broken any laws. You embrace a civil war . . . and you say you're trying to save humanity?" (*Golden Son*, p. 431). Nero's response neatly encapsulates consequentialist thinking: "I do what I need to do to protect the greater good" (*Golden Son*, p. 431).

Darrow asks, "How many would you kill to protect mankind? A billion? Ten?" (*Golden Son*, p. 431). To this Nero replies, "The number doesn't change the necessity . . . Someone must make these choices" (*Golden Son*, p. 431). Like Darrow, Nero takes himself to be making necessary sacrifices to achieve a greater good. They are both attempting to justify their actions based on the goals they are trying to achieve.

Of course, the mere fact that Darrow and Nero both make consequentialist arguments in support of what they do doesn't mean that their actions are justified or even that the two of them are on an equal footing morally. If we assume the truth of consequentialism, everything will come down to whether or not the horrible things that Darrow and Nero each do produce more good overall when all's said and done. However, if we grant that both are pursuing noble goals, then consequentialism may commit us to claiming that both are doing good (or both are doing bad). We can't be sure until we know how things ultimately pan out for the solar system and the human race in *Red Rising*. Regardless, it doesn't seem that consequentialism provides us grounds for thinking that one is a hero and the other a villain.

Duty Is What Matters?

Deontologism is one of the most prominent forms of moral theories (the other most prominent being consequentialism). Rather than construing right and wrong, good and bad, in terms of consequences, deontologism holds that doing your duty is what matters.

The most famous version of deontologism comes to us from the philosopher Immanuel Kant. According to one way of understanding Kantian morality, whether an action is right or wrong depends on whether the action involves treating people as *merely* means to an end or not. For example, asking a friend to help you move a couch, or start a revolution, is treating your friend as a means to your end (moving the couch or starting the revolution), but it isn't treating her as a mere means.

In this case the supporter of Kantian ethics will maintain that you haven't done anything wrong in using your friend as a means of moving your couch. Alternatively, if you force your friend to help you move the couch, you are treating her as a mere means to your end (moving the couch) because you aren't giving her a choice in the matter. According to Kantian ethics, it's always wrong to treat someone as a *mere* means to your ends. So, in this case the supporter of Kantian ethics would claim that you have done something morally wrong because you've treated your friend as a mere means to your end.

Given this basic knowledge of Kantian moral theory, we can easily see that it doesn't give us any grounds for thinking that Darrow is a hero and Nero is a villain. Why? Well, according to Kantian moral theory (or deontology more generally) they're both bloodydamn villains!

When Darrow or Nero sacrifice other people to achieve their personal goals they're treating these people as mere means to their ends. Both have sacrificed others many times, and they have often done this without the people knowing, let alone giving any kind of consent! When people are used in this way they're being treated as mere means to an end.

Even more routinely, both Darrow and Nero lie to others when they deem it necessary. According to Kantian ethics, any time they lie to someone they are treating that person as a mere means to their ends because they aren't respecting the person's autonomy—you know, the person's ability to rationally govern herself. In fact, they're doing what they can to bypass that person's autonomy by giving her false information in an attempt to get her to do what they want. This is treating her as a mere means to getting what they want. Kantian ethics holds that this is wrong—regardless of whether Darrow or Nero is lying to achieve some noble goal.

Since Kantian ethics (and deontologism more generally) holds that consequences aren't what decide the rightness or wrongness of an action, Darrow and Nero both often act wrongly by treating others as mere means to an end. It doesn't matter that they do horrible things in pursuit of noble ends. All that matters on the Kantian perspective is that they do horrible things. Again, this moral theory doesn't provide us with grounds for claiming that Darrow is a hero and Nero is a villain. In fact, Kantian ethics may prompt us to claim that they are both villains!

Virtue and Vice?

The final moral theory that we will consider is virtue ethics. Roughly, virtue ethics holds that what is right or wrong, good or bad, depends upon what a virtuous person would do. According to Aristotle having a virtue requires acting "at the right times, about the right things, toward the right people, for the right end, and in the right way" (*Nicomachean Ethics*, 1106b22–23).

Since Aristotle claims that you must act "for the right end, and in the right way," having the proper motivation seems to be a necessary condition for having a virtue on his view. Given the influence that Aristotle has had on contemporary virtue theories, it is not surprising that contemporary virtue theorists think that possessing a virtue requires having the proper motivation. Perhaps this should be understood to mean not just having the right goals but also being driven by the right motivations and having the right emotional responses to your actions. Maybe here we will find grounds for thinking that Darrow is a hero, and Nero isn't.

Maybe we have at last found a moral theory that draws an important distinction between Darrow and Nero. Although the Reaper of Mars and the Archgovernor of Mars both do horrendous things in pursuit of noble goals, they do so with very different motivations. Throughout all of his many trials and tribulations Darrow continually acts out of love—love for his dead wife, Eo, love for his friends, and eventually love for the peoples of the various Colors.

This is why Darrow struggles so much when he has to lie and mislead those that he cares about. It's also why he's wracked with guilt when he feels compelled to do bad things. He hates that he was forced to kill Julian au Bellona in the Passage, he's distraught when Karnus au Bellona destroys some of his ships at the Academy—not simply because it costs him the contest but because people lose their lives, he "swallows the guilt of leaving hundreds of millions in slavery and personally signing the death warrants of thousands of Sons of Ares to Romulus's police," and so on. Darrow's love and concern for others is his primary motivation. This is true even though at times he is motivated by baser concerns such as his hatred and hubris.

Nero is very different from Darrow when it comes to motivation. Where Darrow is motivated by love, Nero seems solely motivated by pride. As we're told, Nero is "fueled by monstrous, inhuman pride. A pride that goes beyond him . . . It is the pride of a dozen generations of fathers and grandfathers and sisters and brothers, all distilled now into a single brilliant, perfect vessel that bears no failure, abides no flaws" (*Golden Son*, p. 35).

It seems that Nero is fueled by pride to the point where he not only fails to have the proper emotional responses to what he does, he seems incapable of having these responses at all. As Darrow realizes when Nero tells him of his desire to preserve humanity, "There is no morality to him. No goodness . . . He believes he is beyond morality. His aspirations are so grand that he has become inhuman in his desperate desire to preserve humanity" (*Golden Son*, p. 430). It's because of Nero's pride and his complete emotional detachment that he feels no remorse when he does truly horrendous things like beheading his first wife and sending her head to his father-in-law or when he commanded Eo's hanging—"Hang the rusty bitch lest she continue to howl" (*Red Rising*, p. 43). Even at Eo's hanging, the Archgovernor felt no remorse in commanding the death of a woman (a child really) for singing a song; "he doesn't even care enough to watch" (*Red Rising*, p. 44).

So there is an important difference between Darrow and Nero. Although both have noble goals and both do horrible things to achieve those goals, only Darrow has the proper motivation. Darrow is moved to act by love; Nero is moved only by his own inhuman pride.

Hence, at last we may have found grounds to call one a hero and the other a villain. Philosopher Michael Slote is a virtue ethicist who argues that not only is having the proper motivation necessary for an action to be right, it's the only relevant feature. That is, Slote argues that, roughly, an action is right if and only if the person who performs the action has the right motives for performing it. If Slote is correct and we grant that both Darrow and Nero have truly noble goals, we can plausibly maintain that while Darrow's actions are right, Nero's are wrong.

Given Slote's view, Darrow's actions are virtuous—they are right because he has the right motives for performing them. Yet, despite the similarities he has to Darrow, Nero's actions are vicious—they wrong because he has the wrong motivations. And so, we have grounds for claiming what we knew to be correct at the outset: Darrow is a bloodydamn hero, and Nero is a slagging villain!

Kevin McCain

The Road to Hell?

We've seen that virtue ethics, particularly the version defended by Michael Slote, seems to give us clear reasons for thinking that Darrow is a hero and Nero is a villain. This is all well and good, but should we accept Slote's view on things? Is having the right motivation enough to make an action right? Is having the right motivation even necessary for an action to be right?

It seems that the answer to these questions is "No." Let's start with the last question first. It doesn't seem that you have to have the right motivation in order for a given action to be right. Think about when Tactus au Rath refrains from killing Lorn au Arcos's grandchildren. Let's assume that he refrains from killing the children simply because he wants Darrow to accept him as a friend again, or even that he does it simply because he wants to trick Darrow into thinking he has changed when he hasn't. Does the rightness of the action change because of Tactus's motivations? It seems not. It would simply be wrong to kill the children, and refraining from doing so is the right thing to do regardless of the motivation.

Now lets take the other question—is the proper motivation enough to make an action right? It doesn't seem so. Imagine that Tactus had decided to kill Lorn's grandchildren, but he was motivated to do this by good motivations. Perhaps he's motivated by the desire to stop the impending war between Darrow and the Society. Assume that Tactus truly wants to stop the war that Darrow is going to wage and that killing Lorn's grandchildren would help with that goal. This would be a good motivation for killing Lorn's grandchildren, but would that make it right to kill them? No, it's wrong to kill innocent children, pure and simple. Merely having the right motivation isn't on its own enough to make an action right.

While it's clearly true that merely having good intentions or good motivations is not sufficient on its own to make an action right, perhaps there are still grounds here for thinking that Darrow is a hero, and Nero is a villain. It may be that proper motivation is required for some actions to be right even though it isn't necessary in general. It seems there are clear cases where an action is right—Tactus's refraining from killing innocent children, for instance—regardless of motivations. But, perhaps there are some very difficult cases where an action isn't clearly correct apart from motivations.

Maybe Darrow's having a noble goal and being motivated by love makes some of the terrible things he does right, or more plausibly, perhaps his goal and his motivations make the things he does forgivable. Nero has the right sort of goal, but lacks the proper motivations—perhaps that makes what he does unforgivable, if it is. Perhaps this is what makes him a villain.

So, perhaps the reason that Darrow is a hero, and Nero is a villain does come down to their motivations. Maybe Darrow is simply making the best of a very bad situation, and Nero isn't. We can excuse and maybe even applaud Darrow's atrocities because they are motivated by love, and we can condemn Nero's atrocities because they are motivated by his pride. Perhaps that makes one a hero and the other a villain.

Then again, maybe by judging in this way we put too much stock in good intentions. After all, it's long been claimed that good intentions pave the road to Hell.

Maybe, at the end of the day, neither one is a hero?

4
Raising Darrow

TRIP McCROSSIN

"Look into yourself," Dancer urges, as Darrow prepares to set out on Ares's plan to infiltrate and topple the tyrannical rule of the Golds.

The Golds believe themselves to be "the best of humanity," so deserving of the opulent luxury they enjoy on terraformed and colonized planets (and their moons) throughout the solar system. All the while, deep in Mars's mines, Reds have lived in ignorance of the truth for centuries, "slaving, toiling, suffering to create and maintain the foundation of this . . . this empire," as Darrow spits out in disgust, finding truer than he could have imagined what his beloved wife, Eo, had always said—they are "Society's slaves."

Eo martyred herself in resisting this slavery, and in doing so catapulted Darrow into the organized resistance, the Sons of Ares. In pursuit of her dream that someday their people would "break the chains" and "live for more," ultimately, Darrow would become known as the Reaper of Mars. As Darrow reflects on his inner self and prepares to fight to achieve Eo's dream, Dancer tells him, "You are a good man who will have to do bad things."

Darrow's troubled by this, though, not so much by what he'll "have to do," but by what he *wants* to do. "If I am a good man," he worries, "then why do I want to do bad things?" No answer is offered immediately, but an answer unfolds over

the course of the trilogy. In the Society bad things are happening to good people, and worse, they're happening at the
hands of bad people, who are benefiting from doing them.
Darrow wants to do bad things to these bad people to stop
them from doing *their* bad things in the first place. In general, though, what moves him initially is his experience of
the problem of evil—bad things happening to good people,
and good things to bad.

What this may mean for Darrow, to be part of the long
conversation about the problem of evil, helps us to understand better his complex storyline, and perhaps also *our own*.
There's much to draw on, over the course of the trilogy, including, as we begin with here, Harmony's additional and
provocative nickname for him.

Harmony and Darrow, John and Luke

"I'm not dead," Darrow mumbles to himself, repeatedly, in-
credulously. He watched Eo hanged, pulling on her legs to
help end her suffering, as it is customary on Mars to allow
family members to do, where gravity's sadly too weak for the
drop to break the condemned's neck. What they're forbidden
from doing, however, is cutting down and burying their loved
ones afterward. Rotting corpses of the executed remain in
place long after, a warning to all.

Refusing to allow his beloved wife to suffer such indignity,
knowing full well that for this he'll also be hanged, Darrow
sneaks out during the night of her execution, cuts her down,
and buries her in the forest where they'd recently trespassed.
In doing so, he sets in motion the events that lead to his death,
or so he thinks. His uncle had drugged him in advance,
though, so that he'd only appear to die. He awakes not in the
Vale, but alive still, in a shallow grave. "I cannot breathe, cannot move," he panics, as the "earth hugs me till finally I claw
my way free, feel air, gasp oxygen, pant and spit dirt." In effect,
Darrow raises himself from the dead, albeit presumed.

"You're Sons of Ares, aren't you?", Darrow asserts, to one
of the demon-masked who've come to collect him. "And you're

Lazarus," one of them answers, Harmony, as we'll come to know her. Just as Eo being dubbed Persephone can't help but have us think of her in terms of her namesake in Greek mythology, Darrow being dubbed Lazarus can't help but have us think of him in terms of his biblical namesake—namesakes, that is.

Given Darrow's apparent resurrection, it seems most likely that we're meant to recall Lazarus of Bethany, raised from the dead in the New Testament Gospel of John. The resonance seems all the more evident in light of Darrow's second apparent resurrection, roughly two-thirds of the way through the trilogy. But then again, in the Gospel of Luke, we have the parable of a different Lazarus, in Heaven, relating to a rich man, in Hell. Given the story's overarching Red versus Gold storyline, and Eo's "begging for scraps from the master's table" analogy offered in attempting to radicalize Darrow, Luke's parable also resonates powerfully with his plight.

Perhaps Harmony's just joking around, but it seems not. After all, she refers to Darrow as she does as a way of confirming that he's correct, that she is one of the Sons of Ares. The allusion can't help but seem purposeful then. Fortunately, the two parables share a common moral thread.

Lazarus of Bethany is dying, John's parable tells us. His sisters, Martha and Mary, send word to Jesus. Instead of setting out straightaway, however, as they likely expect, and as we likely would as well, he puts the trip off for a few days, knowing that—indeed with the intention that—Lazarus will be several days dead and buried by the time he arrives. Why the delay?, the disciples ask, as again we likely would as well, to which he offers simply that Lazarus's suffering and death are justified by God's glory. Later is better than sooner, that is, as it will allow Jesus to bring him back to life more revealingly than merely back to health.

Before he does, Martha comes along to confront Jesus similarly, that if only he'd arrived sooner, Lazarus would still be alive. To this he famously answers, "I am the resurrection and the life. He who believes in me will live, even though he dies; and whoever lives and believes in me will never die. Do you believe this?" She does, of course, as she confirms, and that's the point. But perhaps, while we may applaud Martha's faith, we may also imagine that if we were her, we might find it no less *reasonable* to wonder, "but I *already* believed, and so wasn't my brother's suffering and death a bit of, well, *overkill*, as it were?" If virtue is what we're after, then even if suffering is somehow helpful, shouldn't we balk nonetheless at a world in which it's otherwise meaningless?

Luke's parable tells us, on the other hand, about the rich man who lives a life of luxury, presumably indifferent to the likes of Lazarus, a beggar at his gate, content with the meager scraps falling from the rich man's table, and of the plights that await them as a result. Eventually they die, of course, and take up residence in Hell and Heaven respectively. And it seems their new accommodations are more or less as expected. Except that the rich man, able to see Lazarus in Heaven, sitting blissfully alongside Abraham, is moved. May Lazarus, he asks, please "dip the tip of his finger in water and cool my tongue, because I am in agony in this fire?" He may not, Abraham answers, as "in your lifetime you received your good things, while Lazarus received bad things, but now he's comforted here and you are in agony."

Good things happen to good people and bad things to bad, *eventually* at least. It also seems that this happens permanently, as a "great chasm has been set in place, so that those who want to go from here to you cannot, nor can anyone cross over from there to us."

But it seems the real problem is that the rich man wants Abraham to take pity not only on him, but also on his five brothers, still living in ignorance of what's befallen him, and so at risk of the same. Who better to set them on the straight and narrow, the rich man figures, than someone who visits from the dead with first-hand knowledge of the importance of this? Again "no," Abraham insists. He'll just have to settle for Moses and the prophets, and besides, it's six of one, half a dozen of the other. "If they do not listen to Moses and the Prophets," Abraham insists, "they will not be convinced even if someone rises from the dead." If he agrees, we may applaud his faith, but again we may imagine that if we were him, we might find it *reasonable* to wonder: "But I *know* they need the better example, because after all, they're *my* brothers." Again, if virtue is what we're after, and it's elusive for the rich man, his brothers, and for the rest of us, then shouldn't we balk at a world in which we're routinely deprived of the exemplary help we need, in avoiding being good people to whom bad things happen?

Harmony dubbing Darrow "Lazarus," again assuming that we think it a serious gesture, sets his struggles throughout the trilogy against individually and institutionally inflicted evil within a broader struggle. Darrow's broader struggle, for him as for his namesakes, is the problem of evil more generally—why, as we saw earlier, do bad things happen to good people, and good things to bad?—why, in other words, are virtue and happiness so unevenly distributed so much of the time?

Darrow as Lazarus as Émile or Candide

The problem of evil is originally primarily a theological problem. Earlier even than our Lazarus's struggles in the New Testament is Job's struggles in the Book of Job, found in the Hebrew Scriptures or the Old Testament. As Milton famously posed the problem in *Paradise Lost*, our experience being what it is, how do we "justify the ways of God" to humanity? However much we may trust in the perfection of God's wisdom, power, and benevolence, and so trust that it's somehow consistent with human suffering, our sense of justice—and so too reason itself—appears unreasonably confounded.

There are hints of this version of the problem in the trilogy: in Harmony dubbing Darrow "Lazarus," of course; in talk of the Vale generally; in Darrow's tenuous relationship to the idea of it more specifically; and more specifically still, in the Jackal's quoting a passage from the second canto of *Paradise Lost*, entitled "Satan's Voyage"—as he murders his father and assumes his reign.

The problem of evil is also a *secular* problem, though, as Susan Neiman has argued. It dates as early as Rousseau's public dispute with Voltaire midway through the eighteenth century. According to the secular version of the problem, human reason is again threatened, but without worrying so much about God, pondering instead: how can we make *reasonable* sense of a world teeming with suffering that appears to *defy* reason? In response, primarily two competing perspectives arose, as Neiman goes on to argue, which have animated philosophical and artistic production since, including Darrow's own storyline. One perspective begins with Rousseau, insisting that "morality demands that we make evil intelligible," the other with Voltaire, insisting that "morality demands that we don't."

To this effect, Voltaire famously offers us Candide, the protagonist of his novella of the same name. Repeatedly appalled by his circumstances, Candide is often consoled by his mentor, Dr. Pangloss, that the world, divinely made, must be the best of all possible ones. His various misfortunes must then be interpreted accordingly—aren't they easily interpretable as contributions to the greater good, he insists, and so in the grander scheme, while we may never know how, as indeed rather fortunate? Until, that is, Candide's *experience* compels him to assert instead that it's not *reason*, but rather simply *work* that distances us from the "three great evils, boredom, vice, and need."

By contrast, Rousseau gives us Émile, the protagonist of his treatise also by the same name. We're not naturally corrupt, Rousseau insists, but rather made so by the long course of our social development. The key to resistance begins, he proposes, with evil made intelligible by the realization that it results from our natural instinct to preserve and promote *ourselves* having steadily overwhelmed our equally natural instinct to act compassionately toward *others*. It ends with the education of at least one uncorrupted adolescent, Émile. This adolescent is ready to enter a newly configured, and so less corrupting, social contract. Rousseau lays out this less-corrupting social contract most famously in the same year *Émile* appeared, in his *Social Contract*.

So what, though, if Harmony dubbing him "Lazarus" sets Darrow's storyline in the context of the problem of evil? And so what if historically the problem's both a theological and a secular concern? And so what if it's the secular version that's at work in the trilogy? And, finally, so what if the secular version has historically these two competing traditions of response, regarding reason's ability to render evil intelligible, one stemming from Rousseau and one from Voltaire?

So what? The *what* that we're allowed, if all of this is true, provocatively it seems, is to ask in which tradition Darrow best fits? Is his response to the problem of evil more in the spirit of Rousseau's, or of Voltaire's, or perhaps in some interesting sense both?

Breaking the Chains, Seeing Them First

Darrow not only resists Eo's plea in the forbidden forest, to "break the chains," to "live for more," but he seems to find it all unintelligible. Such incredulity finds him relating to the evils they suffer more in the spirit of Voltaire than of Rousseau. But Darrow's story is a *developmental* one, of Lazarus-like resurrection and ensuing rebirth.

His "nine months of solitary," for example, before he's to be handed over to Cassius, "is fitting," the Jackal grimly muses, because "war shouldn't make us abandon metaphor." And it's the story of rebirth not just in the performance or unmaking of a carving, but through political awakening. It's in the story of Darrow's resurrection and rebirth, as political awakening, that the spirit of Rousseau arises out of Voltaire's ashes.

The day of his and Eo's arboreal tryst, Darrow the Helldiver helped his clan, the Lambdas, one of twenty-four clans that make up the underground mining colony of Lykos. With his help, they surpassed the quarter's helium-3 yields of all the others, in order to earn the Laurel. Not just a matter of pride, it's a boon to the whole of the clan, in foodstuffs and fineries not included in routine provisions. It's also a matter of justice, as the Laurel's gone to the Gammas for a stretch that seems most easily explained by *in*justice. And the injustice of the system is newly on display when the Laurel goes again to the Gammas, even though with Darrow's draw for the day, the Lambdas had clearly earned it.

Faced with such conspicuous injustice, though, his response is surprisingly subdued. "They won't let us win the Laurel," he reflects, because they "don't care that the math doesn't work," or "that the young scream in protest and the old moan their same tired wisdoms," because it's "just a demonstration of their power," which "keeps the hierarchy in place," as it "keeps us striving, but never conspiring." "Yet despite the disappointment," he continues, "some part of us doesn't blame the Society," but rather "Gamma, who receives the gifts." "A man's only got so much hate," and "when he sees his children's ribs through their shirts while his neighbors line their bellies with meat stews and sugared tarts, it's hard for him to hate anyone but them."

When we hear Eo plead with Darrow, using the immediate injustice to draw his attention to a far broader, she believes equally conspicuous one, we understand that her plea's part of a long and detailed storyline only just beginning to unfold. We might sympathize if Darrow had responded with palpable anxiety, given that hers is the sort of resistance talk that, as a boy, condemned his father to the gallows. What we find much harder to sympathize with, however, is a response that seems now beyond subdued.

He's at first dumbstruck, and then worse, simply incredulous. And we know that discovering the forbidden forest is just the first of two gifts she's promised. And when, disappointed with his response to her plea, she withholds the second, we can't help but worry, and be all the more unforgiving of his response.

Sadly, we find we were right to worry, confronted not only by the lurid injustice of Eo's hanging, but by Darrow's newly disappointing response as well. "I am anger," he reports at first, as she readies to die, "I am hatred," but it's "her choice," and so he's resolute; he'll be "with her to the end." But this takes a turn soon enough. "She left me," he whispers, "just left me," redirecting his anger toward her, in part because the evil's not only insufferable, but incomprehensible. "Musta had a reason," Uncle Narol counters, "not a dumb girl, that one." Narol is trying to console, naturally, but also to teach.

All Darrow can hear in what his uncle's trying to tell him about Eo is that he's "not a man made for affection." He's unable to see in Narol the "mad and brilliant and noble" man his father had claimed, in part because of what he takes to be his father's own foolish revolutionary sacrifice. "You don't know a thing," he insists, "about what she wanted."

And yet, when Darrow chooses to sacrifice himself by cutting Eo down and burying her, performing "the ultimate act of love" he believes, we can't help but side with Narol, in finding him flagrantly neglectful of key parts of her plea. "Because you've a brain," is why she loved him, she'd insisted, adding that he's "not meant to be a martyr," because he "wouldn't see the point." Again, Darrow disappoints. Luckily for Eo, though, Narol's there with his flask and his plan.

Thanks to Narol, Darrow lives, to claw his way out of his shallow grave, so that Dancer can eventually take him to the surface of the planet to witness the lie of the Society. "I do not understand," is all he can think at first, shocked by the "grotesquerie" of Gold culture, which "should not be happening for generations," suddenly laid out before him. Soon enough, though, the scales fall from his eyes. His "life is a lie," he realizes, as he comes to grips with the realization that it's not only real, but has existed for centuries, unbeknownst to Red culture, kept underground and in ignorance, slaving to make it possible. Finally, he's prepared to heed Eo's plea—not to live for her, but for her dream, "*the* dream," that their children "will be born free"—that they'll "be what they like," and "own the land their *father* gave them." But like any other, *the* dream has to be earned. "Eo was right," he realizes, "it comes to violence." What he says, he says to Dancer, but for Eo: "What is my mission?"

Darrow's finally *awake*. He's made the transition from the spirit of Voltaire to the spirit of Rousseau. He understands finally what his uncle tried to teach him, what Dancer has now succeeded in teaching him, which is that even the most grotesque of evils can be infused with meaning. And he's come to this understanding in a manner that's revealing. He doesn't know yet *how* such evils as he's witnessed—Eo's execution—and is witnessing now—Gold abundance wrought from Red slavery—can be made meaningful, but it doesn't matter. In this instant, and for as long as need be, *he*'s the mission—*he*'s the meaning.

From Bad (Gold) Contracts to Good (Rousseauian) Ones

Darrow himself will eventually confirm his Rousseauian turn when he makes his "I would have lived in peace" broadcast in *Morning Star*. This confirmation is all the more evident against the background of his earlier conversation with Victra, recruiting her to the Sons of Ares.

Darrow is raised Lazarus-like from the presumed dead not just once, as noted above, but twice: first early in *Red Rising*, and then again early in *Morning Star*. The intervening storyline—that of *Golden Son*—is of a covert revolutionary strategy gone awry. At the Triumph, convened to recognize him for his successful military campaign against House Bellona, Roque betrays Darrow, horrified to discover him to be the carved Red that he is. His last sights are of Victra dying and the severed and mutilated head of Fitchner, who we've come to know is Ares, and his last thought, "We are undone."

When the storyline resumes in the early chapters of *Morning Star*, Darrow has suffered a year's imprisonment, three months into which the execution of a look-alike is broadcast to the society. Only loyal Sevro is unconvinced, refusing to accept Darrow's death, searching tirelessly. After nine long months, Sevro's finally vindicated, locating him in the Jackal's custody. He dispatches Holiday and her brother Trigg to the rescue.

In the process, Darrow insists that they also rescue Victra, who didn't die after all, but has been the Jackal's prisoner all along as well. Of the three things Darrow eventually insists he needs before returning to the struggle, under

Sevro's leadership as the new Ares, the third is to release Victra from custody—hopefully as the newest Sons of Ares recruit. Darrow imagines he'll have to make amends, at the very least for deceiving her in posing as a Gold, but she wants none of it. "We all enter a certain social contract by living in this Society of ours," she insists. "My people oppress your tiny kind," she clarifies, "you fight back," which is "your right," and it's nothing so grandiose as "good and evil," but rather it's just "fair."

Accepting as she may be of such a bleak social contract, Darrow reminds her that she's also no longer part of it. "The world you know is gone," he pleads, and "you're an outcast from your own people," the problem with "this Society" being that it "pits us against one another." Eo's dream, now Darrow's, is of a different society that doesn't. Instead, society should be based on something nobler. A first step on the new path to realizing the dream, now that he's been "given a second chance at life," is to get Victra to sign on. "You're my friend," he insists, and "I owe you justice," you who "taught me loyalty," and while it takes some additional cajoling, soon enough she's on board.

And, once they've been carved back into their pre-imprisonment warrior selves, and Darrow comes to declare that the end-game's at hand, broadcasting his declaration throughout the Society, it's none other than the first line of Rousseau's *The Social Contact* that he invokes: "Man was born free, but [everywhere] he is in chains." Breaking these chains, however, is only part of Eo's dream, the other being to "live for more," the key to genuine freedom. "I truly believe we choose who we want to be in life," Darrow confesses to Victra, which "isn't preordained," but neither is it irrespective of others around us doing the same.

To be free, and, as such, living for more, is, according to Darrow's pact with Victra, to live in accordance with the virtues of friendship, loyalty, and justice, in such a way that no one person or group is any longer pitted against another.

In more specifically Rousseauian terms, peace comes to us *not only* when the wills we express individually—those, for example, of Red, Obsidian, and Gold siblings Eo and Dio, Ragnar and Sefi, and Adrius and Virginia—are governed by laws that reflect the general wills of the bodies politic they constitute—Red, Obsidian, and Gold cultures respectively; *but also* when the general wills of these bodies politic are governed by laws that reflect the general will of the body politic that together *they* constitute—in our case, the *new* Society of Eo's dream. The trilogy's storyline, as a reflection of the problem of evil, is about an absence of such alignment, the evil that results, and the choice between acquiescence and revulsion, revolution, and the dream of realignment.

Rousseau knew well, as Darrow and the Sons of Ares come to learn, that the process of such realignment is a difficult one, seeing as the general will, ever distinct from any individual one, is ever difficult to discern. Rousseau's vision wasn't to design a utopia and simply move there, but to suffer the slow process of getting ever closer, however far one remains.

"In my youth," Darrow reflects, in the wake of successfully winning the revolution, "I thought I would destroy the Society. Dismantle its customs. Shatter the chains and something new and beautiful would simply grow from the ashes." What he's come now to realize is that it's simply "not how the world works," that a "compromise victory is the best mankind could hope for," but that this is also no small achievement nonetheless. A Gold still rules, for example, but she's also a devoted warrior of the Sons of Ares—Mustang. She is formerly Virginia au Augustus, who's newly anointed as Sovereign, with her fellow warriors' blessing, and who's taken Eo's place at Darrow's side, with whom, he'll soon learn, he has a son, Pax (Latin for 'peace'). "Change will come slower than Dancer or the Sons want," he continues, "but it will come," adding then, in Rousseauian fashion, "so we hope."

Such hope, for Rousseau as for Darrow and the Sons or Ares, comes not only from making evil intelligible, generally speaking, but, as we saw earlier, from doing so by accomplishing two related tasks, as simultaneously as possible.

One task is to accept that evil arises out of a misalignment of individual and general wills, and to set in motion in response a realigning social contract. Successful realignment, however, requires wise leaders—wiser even than Mustang, who is after all a product of misalignment.

The second task, then, is to take advantage of the relative peace of a realigning social contract, to allow for the education of the youth. As this yields a population progressively less dysfunctional over time, its contracts will become progressively more stable over time, which makes education that much more effective, and so on.

Rousseau thought it best to accomplish the latter task as early in life as possible, in the spirit of Émile's education. Mustang's and Darrow's infant son, Pax, provides such an opportunity. What's additionally hopeful about the culmination of the trilogy is not only the revelation of Pax, but that it's immediately preceded by the choice to leave unharmed the deposed Sovereign's grandson, Lysander, an adolescent.

"It's like leaving a pitviper egg under your seat," Sevro worried, because "sooner or later it's gonna hatch." But cooler, more hopeful heads prevail. "I think it's a different world," Darrow insists, and so "we should act like it," and leave him to Cassius—a Gold convert to the Sons of Ares himself—to "raise him right." Just as Mustang and Darrow will tell Pax when he's old enough, Cassius will tell Lysander when he's re-educated enough, of "the dream of Eo, the girl who inspired us to live for more."

After all, if Eo can teach her dream to Darrow, not an easy task, and Darrow can teach it to Cassius, also not an easy task, then each of the rest of us can be taught it as well, however tryingly—to be, like Darrow, "a builder, not just a destroyer."[1]

---

[1] I'd like to thank the editors for their patience and understanding, far above and beyond the call, kindly insisting that they believed, even when I myself was unsure, that in spite of unanticipated turmoil while completing my chapter, I might still have just enough of the Helldiver in me to manage it.

5
The One, the Only, Darrow

KEVIN MCCAIN

Darrow, the hero of the *Red Rising* trilogy, is many things throughout the story that Pierce Brown shares with us. He's a Helldiver of Lykos. He's the Arch-Primus of the Institute of Mars. Darrow is also a standout at the Society's Academy, coming in second overall to that bloodydamn Karnus au Bellona. He's a lancer of House Augustus, eventually becoming Nero au Augustus's chosen heir. But, most of all Darrow is the Reaper of Mars, leader of the Rising.

Throughout his awesome tale Darrow experiences many changes both physical and psychological. Mickey carves him from a Red to a Gold. In the process that magnificent carver enhances Darrow's physical abilities, increases his bone density, even gives him new eyes! Perhaps even more amazingly Darrow undergoes a direct transformation of several of his psychological abilities when Mickey works on his brain building new synapse connections. He is literally made stronger, smarter, and faster as a result of Mickey's carving. All of these incredible transformations are in addition to the astounding emotional and psychological changes that Darrow goes through as he battles to bring down the Society. To say that the Darrow we see at the end of *Morning Star* is a changed man from the Darrow we see at the beginning of *Red Rising* is a bloodydamn understatement!

Thinking of the transformations that Darrow undergoes throughout the trilogy raises an interesting philosophical question: Can Darrow really be the same person after such drastic changes? That is, what makes it so that Darrow the Red Helldiver of Lykos is the same as Darrow the Gold lancer of House Augustus who is the same as Darrow the Colorless victor of the Rising?

This is one of the perennial questions of philosophy, the question of the conditions necessary for someone to persist through time. That is, the question of personal identity.

The Institute before the Academy

Before considering the question of personal identity it'll be helpful to first consider a related philosophical puzzle. This puzzle poses a more general question than that of personal identity: What makes it so that something is the same thing at different times? What are the conditions that allow something to persist through time? One of the most famous ways of describing this sort of puzzle comes to us from Plutarch, though it was likely discussed even earlier. It is what is known as the puzzle of the Ship of Theseus.

To understand the puzzle of the Ship of Theseus let's consider a ship, the *Pax* say. Presumably, when Orion xe Aquarii was captaining the *Pax* after some of the many battles the ship was in, Orion would have to repair the ship. So, parts of the *Pax* would need to be replaced over time. This isn't all that surprising—we do the same thing with our vehicles. Let's imagine that after the Rising Orion continues to captain the *Pax* for many years though. As is natural, she will have to make many repairs to keep the ship in top condition. Over time Orion will replace a large number of pieces of the ship from the guns to the engines to her own seat. If this process continues long enough, eventually the ship that Orion captains will have none of the same parts as the *Pax* that she originally boarded. This prompts a question: is the ship that Orion captains after all of these repairs the same *Pax* that she originally boarded?

Let's make the puzzle even more concrete. Imagine that there is another ship that is similar to the *Pax*; call it the *Quinn*. In fact, let's assume the *Pax* and the *Quinn* are the exact same model of ship, and their parts are interchangeable. As Orion is traveling around the solar system she trades parts with the *Quinn* one part at a time. So, the *Pax* replaces a panel with one from the *Quinn* and vice versa. What happens if this gradual process occurs over a long enough period of time so that the *Pax* is now composed entirely of the parts that were once the *Quinn*, and the *Quinn* is composed entirely of parts that once composed the *Pax*? Is Orion still on the *Pax* or is she on the *Quinn* even though she never got off of her original ship? Is she on neither the *Pax* nor the *Quinn*? Answering these questions is as hard as arm-wrestling an Obsidian!

Fortunately, we don't need to solve this puzzle in order to answer our question about personal identity. But, then why bother with this? The reason is simple: thinking about this helps to warm us up to thinking about the question of personal identity. Importantly, we're now in a position to appreciate that the answer to what makes Darrow the same person over time may not be as straightforward as we first thought, my goodman or goodwoman. Prime?

Who Gives a Bloodydamn?

You might be thinking: Slag this identity stuff! Who cares about the question of personal identity? Although a good Helldiver is quick on his feet, dismissing this question too quickly is akin to running a clawDrill right into a gas pocket. Nonetheless, it's always good to pause briefly and consider why any philosophical question is important. The question of personal identity is no exception.

First of all, Reds believe that loved ones will be waiting for them in the Vale when they die. Darrow mentions that he hopes that all of his friends await him—Red or otherwise. If loved ones do wait, what makes the people who await Darrow in the Vale the same as those he knew when they were alive? Considering the question of personal identity can help shed light on this question. So, our question is important for this reason at least.

There's a more concrete reason for exploring the question of personal identity too though. Darrow's life is extremely interesting, and he's one heck of an exceptional person. However, would the events of Darrow's life be nearly as impressive, if his achievements were really the achievements of several different people? Would Darrow be that impressive if the Helldiver of Lykos is a different person than the Arch-Primus of House Mars who is a different person than the hero of the Rising, and so forth?

No. What makes Darrow so great is *his* many achievements and the many transformations *he* goes through. It's because there's one person who does all of these things that Darrow is so intriguing. It's worth figuring out what makes it the case that it is the same Darrow who does all of the things he's described as doing in the trilogy. That is good reason to explore the question of personal identity!

What's the Burn with Identity?

The first step to considering answers to the question of personal identity is to figure out what the slag the question is even asking. We can distinguish between two kinds of identity: qualitative and numerical. Qualitative identity is a matter of sameness of properties. Basically, this is the sense of identity that we mean when we talk about twins. Twins like Adrius (the Jackal) and Virginia (Mustang) au Augustus are not qualitatively identical, but identical twins are (or, at least they are close to being qualitatively identical).

So, two, or more, distinct things can be qualitatively identical. This is not the sort of identity that we're concerned with, though. After all, it's clear that Darrow the Red is not qualitatively identical with Darrow after Mickey's carving. One is a small Red, the other is a large Gold. One has red eyes; the other has gold eyes. And so on. Heck you're not even qualitatively identical with yourself from a year, a week, or even a day ago!

You have different qualities—likely your hair is at least slightly different, your fingernails are at least slightly different; at a minimum you're different because today you have the quality of being a day older than you were yesterday!

No, howler, we aren't worried about qualitative identity. We are concerned with numerical identity. When we say that x is numerically identical to y we mean that $x = y$. There aren't two things at all. There's just a single thing, and we know it as x and as y. For example, when we say that Ares is identical to Fitchner (sorry for the spoiler, but if you haven't read the trilogy yet, you deserve it!) we aren't saying that there are two people who are very similar. Instead, we're saying that the person known as Ares and the person known as Fitchner are one and the same person. It's this sort of identity that we're interested in.

Hence, our question is about the conditions for numerical identity. What does it take for Darrow the Helldiver of Lykos to be the same person as Darrow the Lancer of House Augustus? What does it take for him to be the same person as Darrow the Reaper of Mars?

Of course, if we were Pixies, we might take the easy way out here and simply say there's nothing that makes them the same—Darrow the Helldiver isn't the same person as Darrow the Reaper. But, whether we are Red or Gold or Blue or any other Color, we are of sterner stuff than that! After all, if we deny that it's actually one person who performed all of the amazing things that Darrow did, he becomes much less of a hero. That is unacceptable. We will pour out an Iron Rain on this question!

In our effort to answer the question of Darrow's identity we will explore some of the major approaches to this problem. In the process we'll gain clarity as to how it is that Darrow at the end of the trilogy is the same person as Darrow the Helldiver at the beginning of the trilogy despite all of his many transformations. Maybe if we're lucky and we dig deep enough, we will walk away with some insight into what makes us the same people over time. Get your clawDrills ready, we're about to dig deep!

Darrow Has the Same Body?

The first sort of answer we might be tempted by is to say that personal identity is a physical relation. The simplest version of this sort of approach would be to claim that Darrow the miner is Darrow the Reaper because he has the same matter throughout.

This, however, is obviously false! Darrow doesn't have the same matter after his body is carved as he did before it was carved. Slag, you don't have the same matter now as you did a couple minutes ago. We lose and replace atoms all the time. So, this answer is a bloodydamn failure.

A better version of this kind of approach claims that it isn't the same matter that matters, it's physical continuity that makes for personal identity. According to this approach what makes Darrow the Red numerically identical to Darrow the Gold is that there is a kind of physical continuity linking the two Darrows.

One version of this approach says that a person just is her body. So, what makes Darrow the same person after the Rising as before has to do with the continuity that there is between his body after the Rising and his body in the past—his body now bears certain causal relations to his body in the past. A similar version of this approach says that Darrow is an animal. That is, he is the thinking animal that exists wherever he is. Eric Olson claims that according to this animalism what makes Darrow the same person throughout his many transformations is that he is the same animal—he's the same living organism after the Rising as he was before it began.

Perhaps our question had an easy answer after all? Slow down, boyo! Things are not as clear-cut as all of that, prime? The first version of this approach, the body version, has some problems. Darrow's body is vastly different after Mickey's carving. He basically gets a new body—different bones, different muscles, different eyes! Is it really correct to say that Darrow has the same body after his carving as he did before? Mickey would faint to hear such words. Despite this, it still seems that Darrow is the same person throughout.

What about animalism? Can it do any better? The answer seems to be "yes." Darrow goes through extreme physical transformations—his brain was directly worked on, his bone density changed, he got new eyes, and so on. He goes through so many physical alterations that it's hard to make the case that he has the same body at all. Nevertheless, one might argue that Darrow still seems to be the same animal, the same living creature, throughout all of these transformations. There is some difficulty with this though—Darrow explains that "the trauma" of his carving "killed me and they had to restart my heart."

Is he the same animal or living organism after dying? Plausibly, he is the same. After all, it seems crazy to think that when Darrow's heart stopped and was restarted some new living organism suddenly sprang into being. Hence, it seems there is one animal that is Darrow the Red, the Reaper of Mars, and one that is Darrow after the Rising. So, we have our answer to the question of personal identity, right? Well, unfortunately, no we don't. There's a major problem lurking like a pitviper here.

The philosopher John Locke's example of the prince and the cobbler poses a major problem for any view of personal identity that claims identity boils down to a physical relation. The gist of this example is that it seems possible that two people could switch bodies without becoming different people.

Consider two very different people, Darrow and his nemesis Adrius, the Jackal. It seems at least possible that perhaps some carver with godlike abilities could transfer Darrow's psychology to the Jackal's body and vice versa. What happens if a carver does this? Darrow wakes up one morning and finds himself in the Jackal's body, and the Jackal wakes up one morning and finds himself in Darrow's body.

Do we say that Darrow just has a really drastic change of psychology—he has the Jackal's memories, thinks he's the Jackal, acts like the Jackal, etc., but is still Darrow? Or, do we say that Darrow and the Jackal switched bodies? Most think the latter is more plausible—Darrow and the Jackal switch bodies in this case. However, if they can switch bodies while still existing, then views which link personal identity to physical things, whether animalism or some other view, have a serious problem. More to the point, if Darrow after he wakes up in the Jackal's body is the same Darrow as the day before in his own body, then linking personal identity to a physical relation has about as much chance of being correct as a Pixie does of winning a razor dual with Lorn au Arcos!

Darrow Has the Same Mind?

As we saw in the previous section, there are some serious problems with linking personal identity to physical relations. Our example of Darrow and the Jackal switching bodies suggests that instead of linking personal identity to physical relations we should understand personal identity to be a matter of psychological features. One overly simplistic version of this approach would be to claim that personal identity is a matter of memories.

So, Darrow is the same after the Rising as he was when he was a Helldiver because he can remember his experiences from that time when he was a Red. This, of course, isn't correct. During the Rising, Darrow can remember experiences from when he was a small child in Lykos. Similarly, it is plausible that twenty years after the Rising Darrow may remember his experiences from the Rising. However, it is also possible that at that time (twenty years after the events of *Morning Star*) Darrow will no longer remember his experiences as a small child in Lykos.

Now we have some slagging weird stuff going on, if we accept this memory view of personal identity! On this view we have to say that the child Darrow is identical to Darrow during the Rising, Darrow during the Rising is identical to Darrow twenty years after the Rising, but the child Darrow isn't identical to Darrow twenty years after the Rising. This amounts to claiming $x = y$ and $y = z$, but $x \neq z$. That's bloody-damn crazy! So, this clearly isn't the way to understand the conditions required for personal identity.

Philosopher Sydney Shoemaker offers a much better version of the psychological approach to personal identity. According to Shoemaker, personal identity isn't a matter of having the same memories. Instead, personal identity is a matter of having psychological continuity—having mental states that are causally connected to one another in the appropriate way. This view avoids the turd in the swillbowl that stinks up the memory view. On the psychological continuity approach, child Darrow is identical to Darrow during the Rising, Darrow during the Rising is identical to Darrow twenty years after the Rising, and child Darrow is identical to Darrow twenty years after the Rising. The reason that these are all the same Darrow is that there is the right sort of causal connection between their mental states. Prime, so far.

The psychological continuity approach also gives the correct result in the case we explored in the previous section where Darrow and Adrius switch bodies. Darrow continues to exist in the Jackal's body after the switch because his mental states are causally connected with his earlier mental states in his own body. So, the psychological continuity approach avoids the problems of the physical approaches as well. This slagging personal identity question is answered, right?

Unfortunately, no. There's a bloodydamn problem lurking for this approach too. Think back to our example where a carver switches Darrow's and the Jackal's bodies. Let's modify this example a bit.

Now instead of swapping bodies a carver simply puts Darrow's psychology into a new body perhaps because Darrow is badly injured. Let's assume that in order to increase the odds of success the carver splits Darrow's brain and puts one half of Darrow's brain into one body and the other half into another body. Prime so far? After this, being the genius carver that he is, the carver is able to get both new bodies to survive. What's more, both of the new bodies function and have Darrow's personality, memory, and psychology. Both individuals think they are Darrow! On the psychological continuity approach it seems that both are Darrow since they have psychological continuity with him. But, this seems to lead to the same sort of bloodydamn problem that we had with the memory approach!

We have three relevant individuals in this case: Darrow, new Darrow 1, and new Darrow 2. On the psychological continuity approach to personal identity Darrow is identical to both new Darrow 1 and new Darrow 2. However, new Darrow 1 and new Darrow 2 are not identical. So, we again have a case where $x = y$ and $y = z$, but $x \neq z$. That's crazier than some of the lines that the Society tries to feed the Low Reds! Slag that. So, there's at least a serious challenge for construing personal identity as a matter of psychological relations.

Darrow Has the Same Soul?

At this point you might be thinking there's a simple answer to this personal identity question. Various religions have given us an answer to the question of what makes someone the same person over time: the soul. So, one might claim that what makes Darrow the same person over time is that he has the same soul.

This response avoids a lot of problems. First, it easily gets the right response in the body swapping case that we discussed above. Darrow is in the Jackal's body, but he's still the same Darrow as before the carving because he has the same soul. Second, it avoids the problems that we mentioned for the psychological approaches too. It doesn't matter if Darrow twenty years after the Rising no longer remembers experiences from when he was a child in Lykos. He's still the same person because he has the same soul. Likewise, we aren't committed to claiming that Darrow is identical to both new Darrow 1 and new Darrow 2. Darrow is identical to whichever of these individuals has his soul. So, if after the carving new Darrow 1 has Darrow's soul, then he is Darrow. If new Darrow 2 has Darrow's soul, then he is Darrow. If neither of them have Darrow's soul, perhaps it departs because of the carving, then neither is actually Darrow.

The soul approach to personal identity provides a tidy solution to the issue of personal identity, a solution that avoids the problems that plague the other approaches. In addition, this approach helps account for the Vale. If there are souls, then it makes sense that one's loved ones could be waiting in the Vale after they die. If there aren't souls, then it's hard to see how Reds can be right about the afterlife. Finally, we're prime, right?

Well, there's one major issue with the soul approach. It's bloodydamn hard to prove that there are such things as souls. After all, you can't see a soul. In fact, since souls are supposed to be immaterial, presumably you can't have any sort of contact with one through any of your senses. In light of this you might be hesitant to accept that there are such things at all. If there are no souls, then the soul approach clearly isn't correct. Again, we're stuck with a tough rock to mine!

Maybe There's No Clear Answer?

There is one final approach to the question of personal identity that we might take. Some philosophers, such as Trenton Merricks, argue that there are no strict conditions that we can spell out for personal identity. They argue that while we might have evidence for thinking that something is numerically identical to something at another time, there are no criteria that must always be satisfied for numerical identity. So, they argue that there's no answer to what makes Darrow the same person over time. Slag! This approach simply says we can't answer the question we set out to answer. That's bloodydamn disappointing!

Rather than accepting this approach, perhaps we should continue to explore the approaches we considered above. Maybe they can be fixed to avoid the problems they face. Or maybe there are other approaches that are yet to be discovered. At any rate, we should explore them before giving up on answering the question—after all, Darrow wouldn't have broken the chains if he gave up at the first sign of trouble!

So, what's our ultimate answer here? Well, even a Peerless Scarred would agree that philosophy can be gorydamn hard at times, goodman! The issue of personal identity is definitely one of the times that philosophy can be quite difficult. But, you might still press—okay, but what's the answer?

At this point, we are clearer about the nature of the question of personal identity, and we are clearer about the major options that have been explored as well as their problems. If you want more of an answer, then you'll have to work through this issue more for yourself. Perhaps you'll shift the paradigm on this issue like Darrow does so often in the trilogy and discover a new approach.

At the end of the day Fitchner's words ring true when it comes to answering the questions that are at the core of what everything is about, such as the question of personal identity, "This is your fight, boyo."

II

Searching for Eo's Dream

6
Driven by Love to Go to War

JOHN V. KARAVITIS

*H*ic sunt leones. "Here be lions."

These are words of both admonishment and encouragement uttered by the Golds of the House of Nero au Augustus, right before a battle is about to begin. Darrow speaks them to Roque right before he prepares his fleet for the final assault among the asteroids against Karnas au Bellona. "The words of our master, Nero au Augustus, ArchGovernor of Mars."

Nero blesses Darrow with these words at the concluding gala of the Summit on Luna. Here, they act as "part challenge, part benediction." After Tactus flees with Octavia au Lune's grandson Lysander, Darrow plans an assault on the *Vanguard's* bridge. Nero, guessing his plan, offers these words as a benediction. Darrow utters them while locked in a spitTube right before the Iron Rain assault on Mars, to encourage his brothers-in-arms. "Be brave. Be brave, and I'll see you on the other side."

It's a curious phrase—words of admonishment, encouragement, benediction, and even challenge. In Dante Alighieri's epic poem *Divine Comedy*, lions were a symbol of *pride*. Given Nero au Augustus, perhaps these words are fitting, then. But the phrase might more readily remind many people of a similar phrase we now associate with early mapmaking: "Here be dragons." This phrase was allegedly used as a reminder to sailors of the possibility of danger whenever they enter into uncharted territory. In reality, cartographers of the ancient Roman and medieval eras used another phrase to denote danger, one you are already familiar with: *Hic sunt leones.*

As Darrow struggles to ascend to the pinnacle of power in the world of the Golds in order to destroy it, he is constantly moving into what are for him uncharted territories. Every person is a variable that he must quickly come to understand and control. Every person Darrow meets has his own agenda in the world of the Golds. Every person represents that much more uncharted crimsondamn territory. Yet it seems that Darrow does all that he does in the name of the girl with the red hair—his dead wife Eo. Darrow appears to be driven by his undying love for her.

But does this really make any sense? Does it make sense to say that anyone could still be in love with someone, let alone be motivated to live a lie for years, long after that person is dead? We see Darrow's thoughts return over and over again to Eo, an echo of his heart as it beats within his carved body. So, is it really love for his dead wife that drives Darrow to live a lie in the world of the Golds as he works toward destroying it? Or, even given the evidence presented plainly before our very eyes by the sole narrator of the *Red Rising* trilogy, could we be mistaken—or perhaps have even been unintentionally misled—about what truly drives Darrow?

If it's truly love that drives Darrow, that would explain a lot. Love is a powerful and humbling emotion. It has brought both joy and grief into people's lives. In its own way, love represents both uncharted territory of and truth for the human soul. In the first two books of the *Red Rising* trilogy, we find a distinct pattern recur. We see Darrow, and many of those close to him, go from love, to loss, to war, to death. We see people driven by love to go to war.

To come to grips with—a powerful, yet nimble, *Helldiver's* grip on—the love that seems to drive Darrrow, indeed, on just what love is, we'll have to carve a course of our own into uncharted territory. Uncharted *philosophical* territory. It's territory replete with a cacophonous chorus of the voices of crimsondamn sophists (slagging wiseguys, the lot of them!) who think they've got it all figured out. So we'll have to be on our toes for any seductive and deceptive ideas that might lead us astray. Luckily for us, we have a battle cry of our own. A battle cry that's been around two and a half millennia, far longer than that of the House of Augustus. So get ready your war face; hold on tight to your razor; take a very deep breath; and repeat after me: *Hic sunt philosophis!* "Here be philosophers!"

Act One: Me and You / The Scene of the Two

"I would have lived in peace. But my enemies brought me war." Darrow begins his narration of the events that drove him from the hot depths of the helium-3 mines to the cold expanse of space with a simple statement. All was well in his world. He had family, friends, a purpose to his life, and the love of a good woman. He knew his place in the grand scheme of things. If not happy, he was at least content. Darrow had it all, or, at least as far as he understood, everything that he could possibly want and get.

That Darrow and Eo were in romantic love is not in dispute. We know both from the time that they spent together, and from the fact that Darrow's thoughts repeatedly return to her throughout the trilogy, that Eo meant everything to him. But is it really the love of Eo and the thirst for revenge for her death that drive Darrow in his quest to destroy the world of the Golds? Although many people reading the trilogy would take this view (and who among us is not enough of a romantic at heart to believe that this is what truly drives Darrow), unfortunately, *Darrow and Eo were never really "in love."* Far from it.

I sense that your hand has just instinctively tightened on the handle of your razor. You may think that I've laid a trap for you. That like a *crimsondamn* Gold, I've betrayed you for my own personal agenda. Fear not, gentle reader. I will explain everything. To do so, I must call forth contemporary French continental philosopher Alain Badiou.

Alain Badiou believes that there are four "truth procedures" that we can use to interrogate the world and to understand it better. These truth procedures are art, science, politics, and love. Although there are probably as many definitions of love as there are philosophers to expound on the subject, Badiou explains what he means by love between two people in *In Praise of Love*.

For Badiou, "Love always starts with an encounter." An "event" occurs. This event is *contingent*, which is a fancy philosopher's word for saying that it was an event that, although it did occur, need not have occurred. That is, you met someone whom you either didn't know or didn't plan on meeting, let alone falling in love with. (Surely you know people who can say that they knew someone for the longest time, and then, out of the blue . . .)

Out of all the things that go on in the world all around us, out of the "multiplicity" of events, perhaps you were lucky enough to meet a person who ended up becoming that special someone. To love this person means going beyond yourself and your self-interests. It's not just all about you anymore and what you want.

You start to see and experience the world from the perspective of another person. Your perspective ceases being your own perspective, and rather becomes "the perspective of difference." Badiou has also referred to this as a "Two scene." This change in perspective is the aim of love, for love is "a singular adventure in the quest for truth about difference." Contemporary Slovenian philosopher Slavoj Žižek agrees with this position. For him, true love comes about when you "discern this radical otherness in the Other."

Given that love leads to seeing the world through another's eyes, and thus to a richer understanding of the world, can we say with confidence that Darrow and Eo were ever really in love? In romantic love, yes. In erotic love, yes. But really, truly, "in love"?

While locked in his Helldiver suit, under pressure both physical and psychological, Darrow's thoughts go to the girl with the red hair, the girl that defines his world, the girl that he loves more than life itself. When he returns to her at the end of a hard day's work, all he wants is to be with her, and for her to be proud of him. And their initial acts and words to each other lead us to believe that they truly are in love.

But it's the conversation between them in the hidden glade that reveals the true nature of their relationship. Eo wants to break free of the constraints of their world. Eo understands that they are nothing better than slaves, kept at the edge of starvation in order to be kept under control. Eo desires a better world, and her speech seems full of rage at Darrow when she talks about their lives. Darrow, on the other hand, completely rejects her view. Darrow does not desire a change in the status quo. For him, to rebel would mean disaster. Obedience as "the better part of humanity" is what he was reminded of earlier in the day by Old Barlow as they were arguing over how to handle an apparent gas pocket in the mine. "Obedience is the highest virtue," he reflected as he headed for the horizonTram after the end of the work day. "There's a nobility to obedience," he tells Eo as they rest in the hidden glade. For Darrow, to live for Eo is enough. For Eo, their lives aren't worth living. "Then you must live for more," she tells him.

Their diametrically opposed perspectives on their world, and each one's refusal to acknowledge or to work through the other's thoughts, mean that Darrow and Eo never participated in a dialogue. Rather, they spoke as if they were each just speaking to themselves. It was not a dialogue; rather, it was two monologues. Refusing to look at the world through the perspective of the other is the key indication that Darrow and Eo were never truly "in love." Romantic love and erotic love, yes, without a doubt. But Darrow and Eo never had "the scene of the two." They were never really "in love."

You may object at this point. But your grip on the handle of your razor has relaxed, which is good. You must be thinking that surely I must be drunk on Uncle Narol's swill, and not be in my right mind. Nevertheless, being in love with another demands that the perspective of the other is taken into consideration. You live with another person, deeply care about that person, and so you end up seeing the world from another's perspective all the time. Seeing the world from another's perspective at the very least informs and enriches your understanding of the world. If your understanding of the world hasn't been enriched, then you can't possibly have entered into and become a part of another person's world. You're still alone.

This is also why Darrow isn't driven by love as he struggles to rise in the world of the Golds. You can't love a phantom. You can't love a memory, which is all that Eo now is. Darrow is simply infatuated with the memory of someone he once loved. And it's also why Darrow and Mustang don't truly fall "in love" until the very end of the trilogy.

At the Institute, as they remain hidden in the forest, nursing each other back to health, they begin to grow together. There's certainly a chance for love as Badiou defines it. But with their training over, they are then separated by their new assignments. Even when Darrow thinks to himself that he is in love with both Eo *and* Mustang, that's never the case. After Darrow reveals the truth about his origins, Mustang reacts in a rage and holds him at gunpoint. So, not only had they never spent enough time together to have a chance to fall in love, their hidden, personal, *unshared* agendas wouldn't have permitted it. Darrow is focused on bringing down the world of the Golds, whereas Mustang will do whatever it takes to keep her family alive.

As Badiou reminds us, "the real subject of a love is the becoming of the couple and not the mere satisfaction of the individuals that are its component parts." Darrow and Mustang finally appear to be on the path to true love by the very end of the trilogy, after both the Sovereign and the Jackal are defeated. It is then that Darrow realizes that they will only be able to rebuild their shattered world *together*. "Only together can we bind these people. Only together can we bring peace."

If Darrow isn't, or can't be, driven by love of another throughout the trilogy, then what's driving him? Has Darrow been *lying* to us all along?

Act Two, Scene One: Death Begets Death Begets Death

"If you are thrown into the deep and do not swim, you will drown . . . So keep swimming, right?" Gentle reader, I've just thrown down my left-hand glove energy shield aegis, in a sense. I've made a serious accusation at the end of the last section, and in truth one even more serious by implication, if you're as cunning as a crimsondamn Gold and can read between the lines.

They say love is desire, but we've just learned that's not the case. Badiou's "Two scene" isn't about desire, but rather learning to see the world from another's perspective. If love doesn't drive Darrow, could it in fact simply be desire of or for something else? To figure this out, let's take a step back and quickly review the facts as we've been told them by Darrow.

Darrow lived through a number of traumatic events, all in quick succession. He lost his wife because she dared to sing a forbidden song, and he was sentenced to death for cutting down her body and burying her. He survived his execution, only to be drafted into the Sons of Ares. His body carved so that he could pass for a Gold, he survived the Institute and joined the House of Nero au Augustus, the same man who had sentenced his wife to death. He's lived as a Gold, loved as a Gold, fought as a Gold, and even killed as a Gold. Throughout all this, his thoughts continually return to his dead wife Eo, and the hope she had for a better future for her people.

One might be led to accept, if not fervently believe, that Darrow is indeed fighting to bring Eo's dream to life. He refers to his efforts as "Eo's dream" on more than one occasion—"because I did it for a dream, for our people." Perhaps Darrow truly does now believe in her dream, which would make his love *agape*. *Agape* is a general, unreciprocated concern for humanity—the highest form of love. It implies selflessness, spirituality, and personal sacrifice. He reflects on the path he is on. "I can give my people a future."

But as I've demonstrated that it's not love of his wife that's really driving Darrow, I'll also demonstrate that, at least through the first two books of the trilogy, *it's not agape.* Unfortunately, it's something rather sinister.

Darrow takes to being a Gold all too well. At the Institute, the Jackal makes Darrow an offer that would guarantee his rise in the world of the Golds. But Darrow will have none of it. "Oh, I want to accept. But then I would have to let the Proctors beat me." Given the choice between a guarantee of success and revenge, he chooses revenge. When Darrow and his forces storm the floating residence of the Proctors, Mount Olympus, he forces himself to feel rage in order to push forward. Darrow's success at capturing Mount Olympus depends on emotion. "I took it with anger and cunning, with passion and rage." When his time at the Institute is over, Darrow acknowledges how much he has become like the Golds. "I'm more like the Iron Golds. The best of the Peerless. Those like the Ancestors. Those who nuked a planet that rose against their rule. What a creature I've become."

To fight Cassius at the concluding gala of the Summit on Luna makes no sense. To fight Cassius *with a razor* is sheer madness, even with Darrow having been trained in the Willow Way by Lorn au Arcos. Darrow denies that he's a Gold, yet he acknowledges a certain kinship with them. "Golds, in many ways, are so like Reds." But he goes beyond kinship, and thinks as a Gold would. "But this is why I was made. To dive into hell." After he storms the bridge of the *Vanguard,* he tells the crewmembers, "My vocation is conquest." Indeed, Darrow believes that *only he can change the world.* When he visits his mother, he tells her, "Someone has to fix all this . . . Someone has to break the chains."

When his closest friends try to counsel Darrow about the negative aspects of his behavior, he refuses to listen. Roque tells Darrow, "You drive friends away as though they were enemies." Darrow even refuses counsel from the woman who could very well take Eo's place in his life. Mustang warns him, "You're not invincible, Darrow. I know you think you are.

But one day you'll find out you aren't as strong as you think you are, and I'll be alone."

What's going on here? Darrow began his journey from the hot depths of the helium-3 mines to the cold expanse of space with a traumatic event that caused him great sorrow and shame. Just a few years later, Darrow now lives his life as someone completely different. Darrow is a lowRed with the body of a Gold. He is self-centered, refuses the counsel of close friends, lies to himself about his motives, is delusional to the point where he believes that he can accomplish anything, and that only he can save the world. He obsessively thinks about his dead wife and her dream of a better world. I believe that, on the face of it, these personality characteristics can without any doubt have a specific label applied to them.

Narcissism.

Act Two, Scene Two: The Root of All Evil— and All Good, Too

Narcissism is defined as extreme self-love, so extreme as to be pathological. Narcissistic behavior is typically driven by anxiety and guilt and shame. You may refuse to believe that this label would apply to Darrow. When you truly love someone, you're supposed to think about them constantly, aren't you? And he is in fact following through on Eo's last wish, which was to see her people set free to claim the world that is rightfully theirs. Isn't this *agape*? How can this be narcissism?

Whether self-love is good or bad depends on degree. Swiss-born French philosopher Jean-Jacques Rousseau (1712–1788) believed that the first person whom one must love is oneself. In the *Discourse on Inequality*, Rousseau describes this self-love, or *amour en soi*, as being absolutely necessary. Self-love drives us to survive in the world, and to even strive to achieve excellence in all that we do. Without the desire for self-preservation, nothing else is possible. In *Émile, or On Education*, Rousseau held that "love of man derived from love of self is the principle of human justice." When we imagine others suffering, we feel their pain. We empathize; and we take pity on them, for their pain could just as easily be ours. In the extreme, self-love becomes *amour propre*. This is vanity and pride, and it is evil.

German social psychologist Erich Fromm (1900–1980) also believed that narcissism and evil are linked. The narcissist is inclined to lie, and to treat others as objects. But the narcissist also lies to himself, which denies him the ability to free himself from his condition. As with Darrow. Narcissism may also lead to fascism, which vividly describes the world of the Golds.

Darrow's constant return to thoughts of his wife and her dream for a better world are the lies that Darrow tells himself in order to deal with his shame at having been unable to prevent his wife's death. Darrow hears what he wants to hear. He wants to believe that he's doing what he's doing for Eo's sake and for his people. But in reality, he's doing it all for himself. He hasn't *intentionally* lied to us. But he *has* lied to us . . . *and to himself*. If Darrow had faced reality, he would have understood that he is blaming himself for that which he could not control. He couldn't control Eo's thoughts and opinions; he couldn't control her decision to sing the forbidden song; and he couldn't stop Nero from ordering her death.

Darrow's descent into narcissism was born of his shame and remorse at his wife's death, but was nurtured by his physical, social, and mental adaptations to live life as a Gold. Darrow's narcissism is in fact a defense mechanism that shields him from his shame at his perceived failure to protect his wife.

In the *Nicomachean Ethics*, Aristotle (384–322 B.C.E.) notes that we become what we habitually do. Darrow lives life as a Gold, with no way back to his life as a lowRed. Throughout the first two books of the trilogy, in his quest to bring down the world of the Golds, Darrow remained trapped in his self-imposed narcissistic prison.

At the beginning of the final book of the trilogy, *Morning Star*, Darrow has been captured, interrogated and tortured, and imprisoned under horrific circumstances by the Jackal. The psychological trauma of having been imprisoned for nine months in the hollow center of the Jackal's stone dinner table shattered Darrow's self-centeredness, his narcissism. While entombed in a womb of stone, Darrow acknowledges, "Man is no island. . . . We need others to tether us to life, to give us a reason to live, to feel. All I have is darkness." The cold, black abyss of his seemingly interminable imprisonment forces Darrow to finally abandon his narcissism and embrace *agape. Darrow is thus reborn into the world, as Eo would have wanted.*

Act Three: To Live to Love to Live to Love . . .

In Book III of the Roman poet Ovid's book *Metamorphoses*, we find the fable of Narcissus and Echo. Echo was a water nymph condemned by the goddess Hera to repeat the last few words that had just been spoken to her. She fell in love with Narcissus, but he rejected her. *He wouldn't listen to her.* Echo wasted away, until all that was left was her voice. Later, Narcissus rests by a pool, and, seeing his reflection in it, falls in love with it. Yet he stays there; and, like Echo, he finally wastes away. In his place grows a flower, which we now call the narcissus.

The meaning of any fable depends on whom you talk to. But we have seen that Darrow initially rejected Eo's dream. Eo's name brings to mind the water nymph Echo. Both couples are associated with a flower (here the haemanthus or "blood blossom"). Eo's song continues to echo both in Darrow's heart and throughout the solar system. And it's not until Darrow is able to willingly shed his narcissism and embrace *agape* that he can succeed in bringing down the world of the Golds. These parallels all serve to reinforce my contention that the main theme of the *Red Rising* trilogy is a warning against the danger of narcissism. "Man is no island . . ."

We desire and are driven to pursue what we do not have. *That's what Life is.* It's true that we cannot escape living with desire. Life wouldn't be Life without desire—desire for survival, for the love of another, for children, for recognition, and even for excellence in what one strives for. But as with all things, desire must be tempered by humility and common sense, lest it get out of control and destroy one's life.

Philosophers have the same desire for fulfillment, only for them, it's to move away from ignorance, from not knowing how or why the world is, to knowing (or at least believing that they know). When it comes to what *love* should mean to us, to our lives, we should let Darrow's hard-won wisdom guide us through the rest of our days on this or any other world:

"Life without love is the worst prison of all."[1]

---

[1] I must offer my sincerest thanks to Professor Bill Martin of the Philosophy Department of DePaul University in Chicago, and fellow student and seeker-of-truth Kasia Kawczynski, with whom I participated in a Badiou study group, Winter Quarter 2015. I had the opportunity to read many of Alain Badiou's works, and our study group's weekly conversations helped me to expand and to enrich my understanding of philosophy.

7
Being for Red

CourtLand Lewis

> Judging whether life is or is not worth living amounts to answering
> the fundamental question of philosophy.
>
> —Albert Camus, *The Myth of Sisyphus*

Who are you? Seriously, think about how you answer this "simple" three-word question.

Do you mention your age, occupation, or where you're from? Do you lie and tell people what you want them to believe, or do you tell them about the type of person you hope to be in the future? Do you mention your name? Do you even know what your name means? The short string of letters that make up your name is more than just the word you put on a "name tag." It's a life story that symbolizes every aspect of your identity.

So, who are you? If you have trouble answering, imagine the difficulties Darrow might face answering. Is he a Red, a Gold, some hybrid, a god, a rebel, a savior, or none of the above?

It's amazing how what appears to be such a simple question can be so difficult. Darrow starts out as a malnourished Helldiver living underground, becomes a healthy super-human fighting-machine on the verge of destroying a society, and ends with his health, family, and freedom.

Parts of his Redness remain throughout the story, seen in his memories and when he visits his mother at the end of

Golden Son, but except for the occasional "bloodydamn" mistake, he's more Gold than any other color. This creates a psychological tension between his original goal to avenge Eo's death, by destroying Gold society, and his experience of love and friendship as part of that society.

Would you be surprised to find out that you encounter a similar tension throughout your entire life? Though it might not seem as extreme as Darrow's tumultuous existence, it's every bit as challenging as surviving the Institute. The biggest difference is that you've gotten used to it over the years. You've internalized the struggle. From the time you were born, to the time you find yourself reading these words, you've trained yourself to interact with the world in a consistent and "normal" way, even though you're constantly torn between competing psychological forces. Don't believe me? Well, maybe you will after I've done some brain and bonepeeling. Mickey taught me all his tricks, so I hope you're ready.

Slagging Self

One way to answer the question "Who are you?" is to talk about personal identity, and to an extent it can't be avoided. A more interesting way to answer the question is to focus on our existential nature. In other words, what does it mean for us to exist as a person engaged in living? By focusing on our existential nature, we not only gain a clearer picture of our existential plight as individuals, but we also gain a better understanding of Darrow's existence in the *Red Rising* trilogy. The best place, then, to start is by determining whether our "self" exists.

One way in which to think of the self is to equate it with the soul. The concept of the soul appears in many cultures throughout history, and even though there are many ways to conceptualize the nature of a soul, it has most commonly been considered the non-physical locus of our personal identity. By the time of the Ancient Greeks and Socrates, the concept of a soul expanded to include not only personal identity, but was considered the true self of a person, the non-physical spiritual self, connected to and in control of our physical body.

Throughout Plato's middle and late dialogues, Socrates argues that each person has a soul—a unique, non-physical, immortal self. In fact, the soul plays such a necessary role in Plato's theory of knowledge that, in *Meno*, Socrates maintains that the soul is required for all knowledge, and in *Phaedo*, he provides several arguments to show how the soul survives death, exists for a time in a realm of pure knowledge and understanding, and, unless you have learned to overcome the desires of the flesh, eventually returns to inhabit another earthly body. We also learn in these dialogues that the soul is directed towards the divine, seeks wisdom and understanding, and is designed to rule the body—the body being a mere slave to earthly pleasures like comfort, food, drink, and of course, carnal interactions.

Socrates might say, we observe Darrow's soul when he's considering how he—the Darrow "inside"—should act around Golds and whom he should trust with the knowledge that his soul is much different than his Gold body suggests. Should he tell Mustang he's a Red? Should he trust Jackal? Socrates would say that when Darrow uses his intellect to guide his body, his soul is in charge, but when he throws himself into dangerous and suicidal missions, whether it's crashing his escape pod into Karnus's ship, or making love to Mustang, the "mad furious master" of his body is commanding his soul.

Does the fact that Darrow thinks imply he has a soul? It depends on who you ask. René Descartes would answer "Yes." For Descartes, the fundamental truth of human existence is that we, as thinking things, exist. As he illustrates in *Meditations on First Philosophy*, it's possible to doubt every aspect of existence, from perceptual experience to physics and math, but when all's said and done, there must be something doing the thinking. An idea only exists if there's a mind to think it, so since our mind has ideas, we (as thinking things) must exist. Descartes referred to our thinking mind as our soul, our consciousness, our *self*. After proving a soul exists, Descartes goes on to argue for the existence of a Perfect Being and material objects, and just like Socrates, Descartes maintained that the purpose of the soul was to control the body with reason and understanding.

We can also answer "No." David Hume, for instance, would say that thinking and awareness don't imply the existence of a soul. Unlike Socrates and Descartes, who privileged reason over experience, Hume refused to make claims of knowing something to exist, unless such beliefs could be traced back to empirical experience. Hume would say that Darrow's thinking is merely proof that there are certain mental activities occurring, and that the concept of a soul comes simply from our awareness of these activities. We don't see Darrow's soul when he's thinking, we simply see a series of thought processes.

The same thing occurs with us. Imagine you're deciding whether or not to sing Eo's song. It feels like there's some independent thinking thing above and beyond your body and brain doing the thinking, but all that's really happening is that your mental processes have become the object of your mental processes. In other words, you perceive that you're thinking. The same thing occurs when you all of a sudden perceive the sensation of the clothes you're wearing. When you wear clothes, your body is constantly *sensing* them, but you don't always take time to *perceive* them. Every once in a while, however, you perceive your body sensing your clothes, and now that you're thinking about it, you're perceiving the mental process of perceiving your clothes. As a result, your brain puts these ideas and perceptions together, which then leads to a belief in a personal soul or self. According to Hume, we never actually experience a soul, and since we can't know what we can't experience, we can't know we have a soul. So, for Hume, Darrow's thinking doesn't imply he has a soul, after all.

Look in the Box

The difficulty of determining whether your soul exists is that it is by definition a thing that's *unobservable* with the senses. Testing the existence of *observable* things is easy. Are there pitvipers on Darrow's Mars? Yes, and we know they exist because they plague the Reds who mine the planet. Do humans have a brain? Yes, and if we wanted to be certain we could examine one of the corpses that Darrow creates. Do humans have a soul? We could examine the same corpse, but we would never find a soul. Yet, due to the nature of a soul, as an unobservable thing, we shouldn't be surprised at this result. All of our perceptual abilities, and science itself, is designed to investigate observable, not unobservable things. So, if we're looking for an actual physical soul, we're approaching the problem from the wrong direction.

One approach to finding unobservable things like the soul is to look for its effects. Events have causes, so if there's an event that can only be caused by a soul, then there must be a soul. Like the wind, you can't see it, but you can feel and see its effects; so you know it exists. On one level, humans are simply blood and guts, like all animals. Yet, humans are markedly different than most other animals. For one, humans are capable of being *persons*. I don't mean 'person' in the legal sense often used in public debates concerning laws protecting the unborn and animals. I mean 'person' in the original sense of the word, as having a persona, of being a rational entity with a character (your persona) that chooses to act in certain ways.

The moral sense of the word is commonly tied to the concept of a soul, because 'the soul' refers to a unique, autonomous person, which is why we hold moral *persons* responsible for the choices they make. For instance, the sea monsters that kill any poor Obsidians trying to escape aren't morally responsible because they act from a non-rational, instinctual drive to eat, but Aja is morally responsible for carrying out the cruel wishes of the Sovereign, because she knows (or should know) that killing innocent people—no matter the color—is wrong. Since what separates humans and animals can't be merely blood and bone, it must be something, so far, unseen—the soul. Couple this belief with what for many appears to be the constant experience of a personal soul, and you arrive at the conclusion that a soul exists.

For close to two centuries, psychology has studied the human persona, or psyche. Though we could examine many psychologists, Sigmund Freud serves as a good test subject for discussing the soul, even if there are disagreements regarding what he believed about the soul. Though currently out of vogue, Freud compiled an impressive amount of psychoanalytic data to support the belief in a soul. Referred to as the Self, Freud hypothesized that the Self arises from the tension between the internal animalistic nature of humans and the external social pressures of society.

Donald Palmer amusingly summarizes Freud's understanding of our animalistic urges—our Id—by suggesting that humans are driven by their desire for three Fs: Food, Fighting, and Fornicating. Might sound like one of Jackal's tamer parties, but most real-life societies don't allow people to go around acting like Golds and treating everyone else like Pinks—even if that's what we desperately want. So, to ensure we're able to effectively participate in society, the ethical portion of our psyche—our Superego—steps in to keep our Id in check. The result is the ego, an often *scarred* and fragile personality. Though couched in psychological terms, the ego serves as a twenty-first century soul.

Freud's position is currently unfashionable, but one person who disagreed with him early on was Jean-Paul Sartre. Like Hume, Sartre refused to believe in the existence of things unseen. Instead of relying on some unseen soul or ego, Sartre maintained that human psychology could be easily explained in terms of our normal perceptual abilities. To fully understand Sartre's explanation we need to dig deep into both his philosophical position and Darrow's struggles as a hybrid Red-Gold.

Darrow for Himself and Others

Darrow struggles with who he is and how others see him throughout his post-transformation existence as a Gold. It's not merely that his inner animalistic desires, or his Red-self needs to be put in check by his Superego. No, it's much deeper and more complicated than a Freudian interpretation of the self suggests. Darrow struggles with the fact that on the inside he's one person, on the outside he's another, and when others look at him, they're not only incapable of seeing his true self, but they constantly remind him of his weaknesses. Like Darrow, we all encounter the same struggle, and it's a struggle nicely described by Sartre.

To paraphrase Sartre, "You are what you are not, and you are not what you are." This sums up nicely the psychological angst in which we all find ourselves. For Sartre, there's a psychological disconnect between your physical self and how you perceive your self. Your physical self is the facts of your existence, what Sartre calls the "being-in-itself." These include your height, weight, date of birth, and the many other things which describe your body's physical existence.

Sartre notes, however, that we never see ourselves as simply the facts of our body. We always see ourselves in terms of the future, of what we're striving to become. We create a narrative that always portrays our self in terms of what we hope to become—Sartre calls this internal image of the self the "being-for-itself." For instance, Darrow is physically a Gold, but he doesn't see himself as a Gold. He sees himself as the one who wins at the Institute, a Peerless Scarred, in charge of his own fleet, and the destroyer of Gold society. We constantly do the same. We don't imagine ourselves as the person we are now, but we imagine ourselves in terms of who we want to be, and we define ourselves as that future person. You're not simply the student, you're a graduate; you're not simply a graduate, you're a person with a job; and so on. As a result, "You are what you are not," because you see yourself as different from the physical thing you are.

As if two selves weren't enough, there's a third self that causes even more stress—the "being-for-others." The being-for-others occurs when we notice "the Look" of others, which heightens our awareness of our two selfs. The tension between who you are and who you want to be is often stressful, but it can be overwhelming. Look at the turmoil it causes Darrow in *Golden Son*, when he's prepared to blow himself up, along with many of the most important members of Gold society.

When we see someone looking at us, or even feel or imagine someone else gazing at us, we act differently, often ashamed. We feel vulnerable and weak because we're both reminded of how fragile we are and fear people seeing through the façade of the external self we've created. Sartre has many wonderful examples peppered throughout *Being and Nothingness*, but Darrow provides many of his own. As a Red, he just wants to live peacefully with his wife Eo, but she sees him in a different way, as the savior of their people. As a Gold, he constantly worries that Eo would be disappointed in his decisions, especially when it comes to his love for Mustang. He agonizes over his "friends," since all he's done is lie to them. He's embarrassed that he finds Victra attractive, and he desperately wants to be a brother to Cassius. In fact, the only people he's comfortable around are Sevro, Mickey, Ragnar, and a few others he's been honest with, but even with them, his life-as-a-lie makes him distrustful and secretive.

When we recognize that we all suffer from the tension of these three psychological components, we begin to understand the difficulties we and Darrow face on a daily basis. What's even more fascinating about Sartre's account is that it doesn't require the existence of a non-physical soul. As Hume suggests, the idea of a soul arises merely from the fact that we're aware of our perceptual abilities and that the look from others makes us imagine a self above and beyond our physical existence. Of course, the self isn't the only thing we create due to the look of others. In fact, most of our lives seem to be created fictions designed to protect us from these existential truths.

Prime Freedom and Gory Guardrails

Sartre is an existentialist. In fact, he popularized the term 'existentialism', defined as the belief that "existence precedes essence." Objects are created, based on the idea of the creator.

The creator's idea determines the essence of a thing. For instance, the razor weapon used by Golds was created with the purpose of defending and killing. It can be used for other purposes, like as a fashion statement worn around the arm, but its fundamental essence is a weapon—it can't just decide to be something else.

For Sartre, humans aren't the result of a creator's idea. We're born through a process of natural causes, so we're born without an essence. Our essence is only the result of existing and making choices in the world. Sartre, then, would answer our original question "Who are you?" by saying, "You are the person that results from the decisions you make." Don't be fooled into believing this makes things any easier. As Darrow and the other characters of *Red Rising* illustrate, making decisions consistent with "who you are" is far from easy, and for some, impossible.

To fully understand the implications of an existential self, let's start from the beginning. When we first meet Darrow, he's a Lambda Helldiver, trying to win the Laurel for his clan. With the possibility of rupturing a gas pocket, Darrow is hyper-aware that what he's doing could cause his death. He recognizes the "smell of death," and it excites him. Even so, he pulls back, knowing full well he could push forward to oblivion.

You experience the same feeling when you stand on the edge of a cliff. You realize that you have complete control over life and death; that it takes only one more step to oblivion; and the fear that bubbles up in the pit of your stomach, or yells in the back of your head, makes you take a step back. This is the realization of extreme freedom over your life—and death! You can either embrace it or run from it. To run from it is to live in "bad faith."

Bad faith occurs when we act in ways that run counter to who we are as individuals, in order to ignore both our own desires and fears, and meet the expectations of others. Some of Darrow's machismo as a Red is the result of doing what others expect of him. The fact that he listens to his uncle, instead of continuing to drill appears to be an example of bad faith. He wants to continue drilling, but he uses Eo and his uncle as excuses to stop. He would love to stomp Ugly Dan into the ground, but he rationalizes a set of excuses that prevent him from doing so. You might ask if this is just Darrow's rational self trumping his emotions, but for Sartre, it's merely an excuse, if what he really wants to do is squash Ugly Dan.

Darrow's struggle with bad faith is a major theme throughout the series. In *Golden Son*, he comes up with excuses for why he can't have Mustang or why he can't be honest with Roque. One of the most prominent themes throughout the *Red Rising* trilogy is his dream of a better life in the Vale, where good Reds go when they die. The Vale allows Darrow an excuse to not act or try to change the status quo. It gives him a feeling that justice will be served in the next life, since Golds can't go to the Vale. It comforts him when Eo is hanged, helping him avoid the truth that he's lost his wife forever. All of these excuses are what Sartre would call "guardrails" that "protect" us from being free. By the time we reach *Morning Star*, the guardrail of the Vale is shattered, and even though he'd like for it to be real, he knows that hope is only found in the living.

Freedom is one of the scariest features of human existence. It's something we claim to want above all else, yet when given freedom, we don't know what to do with it. To avoid freedom, we often fill our lives with guardrails—distractions and excuses why we can't or don't want to do something. What prevents Darrow from staying with Mustang, instead of going to the Academy? He might cite an obligation to continue his mission, but that's only an excuse, if he truly only wants to be with Mustang. If he truly wanted to be in the Academy, then his opining for Mustang seems to be the construction of a guardrail for some future failing. He has the power to choose either future, and though such decisions are difficult, he must make the one he wants and accept the consequences of his choice; for he's ultimately the only one responsible for his decisions. If Ragnar came up to you and said, "Give all your money to the poor, or I will crush your head," it's still up to you whether or not you give your money to the poor. Sure, Ragnar's threat limits your options, but you still have the freedom to choose. The choice you make, then, determines who you are.

Even though the Golden Darrow was created by Mickey, the Red Darrow is still the one in charge. The scrawny Hell-diver who didn't panic while he cut himself out of the mines of Mars in *Red Rising* is the same Peerless Scarred who didn't panic as he cut himself out of his armor at the bottom of the river in *Golden Son*, and allowed himself to be captured to finally bring down the Sovereign, and by extension the corrupt Gold system.

Wisdom Is Found in the Heart

Thankfully, most of our decisions are not as dire as those faced by Darrow. Yet, when all's said and done, whether we have a non-physical self called a soul, or we're a self that results from our complex perceptual abilities, our decisions have the same devastating influence over who we are.

We can choose to live a life in bad faith, where we merely do what others want and expect. If we choose this life, we run the risk of never achieving our true potential, of being bored, miserable, and depressed; but most of all, we run the risk of never developing a self, enriched by living life to its fullest. If we only do what others expect of us, we truly are *merely* an actor on the stage of life. We become a character in someone else's story, and we never write our own. We're like Ragnar before Darrow teaches him to be free. In other words, we're a slave.

When you answer the question "Who are you?", do you want to say, "I'm a slave"? If you're not actively taking advantage of your freedom, examining and overcoming the guardrails that enslave you, then a slave is what you are. If you want to be more than a slave, then you must take control of your freedom.

Will it be easy? No! Was it easy for Darrow, Eo, Ragnar, Fitchner, Mustang, Sevro, Cassius, or any of the others that dared to be free? No! Some people will fear you, you revolutionary. Some will want to stop you, you golden child. And if you're lucky, a few will want to join you, you reaper.

Choosing to be free is as scary as being part of the Iron Rain, but if you want to be alive and free, then there really is no other option. Know thyself, you morning star!

8
Living for More

KEVIN MCCAIN

Live for more. That's what Eo tells Darrow. Throughout the *Red Rising* trilogy Darrow continually reminds himself that he must live for more, and so he does. But, does living for more give Darrow's life genuine meaning? Answering this question amounts to answering one of the deepest questions of philosophy, or of life in general: What is the meaning of life?

Unfortunately, the question of life's meaning can be an extremely tough question to answer. In fact, it can be difficult to figure out what the question is even asking! So, what are we asking when we ask about the meaning of life? This question is ambiguous. On the one hand we might be asking about what philosopher Susan Wolf calls meaning *of* life. On the other hand we might be asking about what she calls meaning *in* life. The first question—what is the meaning *of* life?— is asking: why is there something rather than nothing? Or perhaps more specifically, why do we exist? The second question—is there meaning *in* life?—is asking a more narrow question: what does it take for an individual's life to be meaningful?

Meaning of Life

The first way of understanding the question of life's meaning seems to have a straightforward answer: it depends! Whether there's a reason for why the humans (whether they're the same species as us may be debatable, but they're close enough!) in the world of the Society exist or not depends on whether there is a creator. After all, if there's no creator, then humans of all colors from Gold to Red are simply the result of random cosmic forces. Without a creator there's no particular reason for the human race to exist—it's simply a happy, or unhappy (depending on your viewpoint), accident that the human race ever came about. So, whether human existence as a whole is meaningful depends on whether there's a creator of the human race.

Although a creator seems to be necessary for life to be meaningful, it doesn't seem to be sufficient for giving life meaning. For example, if there's a creator in the world of the *Red Rising* trilogy, but this creator made humans by mistake, then it doesn't seem that human life is meaningful. After all, being an unintentional mistake doesn't seem to confer a purpose or meaning on human existence.

And yet it seems that intentional creation isn't enough on its own to bestow meaning on human life. Even if a creator intentionally created humans, if the creation didn't involve any particular plan or purpose for humans or creating them, it still seems that human life as a whole is meaningless. In light of this, it's apparent that not just any creator will do. In order for human life as a whole to be meaningful, it must be the result of the intentional and deliberate actions of an interested creator implementing a plan. This may seem like a fairly stiff order; however, a being (or beings) capable of creating the humans that exist in the Society could easily engage in intentional and deliberate action. But, this leaves us with an important question: is there such a creator in the world of the *Red Rising* trilogy?

Alas, no explicit answer to this question is given. Nonetheless, if the various Colors of the Society are correct, it seems that the answer is "No." We learn of the religions (or lack thereof) of primarily just three Colors, the Reds, Golds, and Obsidians. While Whites are the priests and priestesses of the Society, we're told very little about their thoughts and beliefs. In fact, Whites seem to be predominately focused on presiding over functions, which they apparently often do in a longwinded, droning fashion. Whites also arbitrate justice and push the Society's philosophy, but they don't seem to actually provide any real religious guidance or information about the presence/absence of a creator. So, we must look to the three Colors that we know more about.

Is There a Creator?

Let's start at the top of the pyramid. Golds seem irreligious on the whole. They have no afterlife, instead "this life is their heaven" (*Golden Son*, p. 114). Darrow tells us what waits for Golds when they die: "only darkness" (p. 124). "When they perish, their flesh withers and their name and deeds linger till time sweeps them away. And that is all" (p. 182). After all, "the Golds have no God" (p. 328). Nero au Augustus clearly states the view of Golds:

> The universe does not notice us . . . There is no supreme being waiting to end existence when the last man breathes his final breath. Man will end. That is the fact accepted, but never discussed. And the universe will continue without care. (p. 430)

Hence, if the Golds are correct, the answer to our question is negative: there is no meaning to human existence.

What about Obsidians? They have a religion and gods. But, theirs is a manufactured religion of false gods. The Golds "took their history, took their technology, wiped out a generation, and gave their race to the poles of planets, the religion of the Norse, and told them that we [Golds] were their gods" (p. 196). There's no evidence of a genuine creator to be found among the Obsidians. This is something that the Obsidians themselves learned when Sefi and several of the Valkyrie helped Darrow and Mustang capture Asgard. In the process they even killed some of the Golds posing as gods. Sefi even refers to the Rising as Darrow's "war against false gods" (*Morning Star*, p. 264). There's no evidence of a genuine creator to be found among the religion of the Obsidians.

Finally, we come to the bottom of the Society's pyramid: Reds. Reds have religion and songs that teach them about this religion. They have an afterlife and someone important in that afterlife. Reds have the Vale and the Old Man. The Vale is a "green vale where woodfire smoke and the scent of stews thicken the air . . . the mist there is fresh and the flowers sweet" (*Red Rising*, p. 53). "In the Vale there is no pain" (*Morning Star*, p. 54). It is a place where "we see our loved ones when we pass on" (*Red Rising*, p. 53). When Darrow is facing Adrius, the Jackal, in their final showdown he recalls to himself those who will meet him in the Vale, "she [Eo] waits for me now at the end of the cobbled road, as Narol does, as Pax and Ragnar and Quinn, and I hope, Roque, Lorn, Tactus and the rest" (*Morning Star*, p. 500). If the Reds are correct, then there is an afterlife where families are reunited and pain is no more. This sounds great, but it alone isn't enough to make human existence meaningful. Without a creator, the existence of the Vale and Reds' afterlives (and other Colors', if Darrow is correct about who waits for him) are just as accidental as the rest of human life in the world of *Red Rising*.

Yet, in the Vale "there is an Old Man with dew on his cap who makes safe the vale," and this Old Man stands "with our kin waiting for us along a stone road beside which sheep graze" (*Red Rising*, p. 53). What of this Old Man though? The Old Man "does not help us in this life. He merely waits to shepherd and guard us in the next" (*Golden Son*, p. 329). Well, he sounds like a nice enough fellow since he shepherds and guards people in the afterlife, but he doesn't sound like a creator. If there is no creator, then the Old Man's existence is just as random and meaningless as anything else. Yet again, we don't get evidence of a creator from the religion of the Reds.

In sum, there doesn't appear to be any evidence of a creator in the world of *Red Rising*. If there is no creator, this gives us a disappointingly negative answer to the question "What is the meaning of life?" There isn't one; human existence is meaningless. And, you thought you were bummed out when Fitchner lost his head, boyo!

In light of this depressing answer to the question of life's meaning it might be tempting to think that individual human lives are meaningless too. That is, we might assume that because there is no meaning *of* life that there is no meaning *in* life either. It would be a mistake to jump to this conclusion though—perhaps not as foolish as agreeing to a razor dual with Lorn au Arcos, but a mistake nevertheless. The question of the meaning of life is distinct from the question of what it takes to have meaning in life. Even if there is no purpose or reason that humans as a species exist, and so human life as a whole is meaningless, it doesn't follow that individual lives are meaningless. It may be that despite the meaninglessness of human existence as a whole, a person can still have a meaningful life. So, we shouldn't assume that the answer to "Is there meaning in life?" is also negative. Let's explore this question by focusing on the life of Darrow of Lykos, the Reaper of Mars and hero of the Rising. If anyone in the world of *Red Rising* has a meaningful life, the man who brought the Society to its knees and freed the Reds does!

Meaning in Life

When we think about the question of meaning in Darrow's life we're asking whether his life is meaningful. Before we can appreciate the answer to this question though we must first get clear on what it takes for a life to be meaningful in general. So, come Helldivers, let's dig into this question!

Philosopher Garrett Thomson helpfully distinguishes three broad answers to this question. He terms them: *supernaturalism*, *pessimistic naturalism*, and *optimistic naturalism*. The simplest way to understand these views is in terms of their responses to three claims:

1. **God exists.**

2. **God, and only God, gives meaning to individuals' lives.**

3. **Individuals' lives have meaning.**

Supernaturalism is committed to the truth of all three claims. Supernaturalism is the view that meaning in life comes from God alone, there is a God, and God gives individual human lives their meaning.

Next, pessimistic naturalism like supernaturalism is committed to the truth of 2, but it holds 1 and 3 to be false. So, pessimistic naturalism involves accepting that only God can give meaning to an individual's life while denying that God exists. This leads straightforwardly to the conclusion that individual lives are meaningless.

Finally, optimistic naturalism differs from both supernaturalism and pessimistic naturalism in that on this view 2 is false. Optimistic naturalism is committed to the truth of 3 and is agnostic about 1. Hence, optimistic naturalism is the view that at least some individuals have meaningful lives, and the meaning in these lives is not dependent on God— whether or not God in fact exists.

Supernaturalism and the Life of Darrow

Supernaturalism says that meaning in life depends upon God, and God does in fact exist and gives meaning to lives. If this view is correct, then it's plausible that Darrow's life is meaningful. Unfortunately, as we noted earlier, there does not seem to be a creator-God in the world of *Red Rising*. If there is no God in the universe of the Society, then supernaturalism is false. If supernaturalism is false, it cannot tell us whether Darrow's life is meaningful or not. Thus, we need to look elsewhere for an answer to our question. Fortunately, we have two more broad approaches to this question to explore.

Pessimistic Naturalism and the Life of Darrow

Nero au Augustus's conversation with Darrow nicely expresses pessimistic naturalism, "The universe does not notice us . . . There is no supreme being waiting to end existence when the last man breathes his final breath. Man will end. That is the fact accepted, but never discussed. And the universe will continue without care" (*Golden Son*, p. 430). It's not hard to see why this view is called "pessimistic"! According to pessimistic naturalism, there is no God but without God no one's life has meaning. Hence, Darrow's life is meaningless just like everyone else's, if pessimistic naturalism is true.

What can one do in the face of this pessimism? One approach, defended by the philosopher Albert Camus in his *The Myth of Sisyphus* and embraced by Karnus au Bellona, is to respond with defiance. We can continue to live in spite of the meaninglessness of our lives. Darrow tells Karnus that "pride is just a shout into the wind" (*Golden Son*, p. 97). Karnus responds in a way that might make Camus proud, "All that we have is that shout in the wind" because "I will die. You will die. We will all die and the universe will carry on without care." Consequently, Karnus claims "pride is the only thing" (*Golden Son*, p. 97). Now, while he does append to this that there's one other item of worth in life, "women," Karnus is ultimately expressing the sort of defiance in the face of meaningless that Camus advocates. Another approach is to live our meaningless lives with a sense of "irony instead of heroism or despair," as philosopher Thomas Nagel suggests ("The Absurd", p. 27).

Is this really all there is though? If there's no creator in the *Red Rising* universe, must we say that Darrow's life is meaningless? Or, might his living for more give meaning to his life? Let's turn our attention to this final option by exploring two key kinds of optimistic naturalism: subjectivism and objectivism.

Subjectivism and the Life of Darrow

The first kind of optimistic naturalism denies that God must exist in order for an individual's life to be meaningful. Instead, subjectivism holds that an individual's life is meaningful insofar as it is enjoyed by that individual. As philosopher Richard Taylor expresses the view, "The point of living is simply to be living, in the manner that it is your nature to be living" (*Good and Evil*, p. 334). The idea here is that an individual's life is meaningful just in case she is engaged in activities that she enjoys—regardless of what those activities are.

Taylor introduces subjectivism by discussing the Greek myth of Sisyphus. According to this myth, the gods punish Sisyphus by making him eternally roll a heavy stone up a hill. Right when Sisyphus gets the stone almost to the top of the hill it rolls back down, and he has to start the process all over. What a horrible and meaningless activity to spend eternity performing! Taylor, however, asks us to imagine a modification of the myth. He asks us to imagine that Sisyphus loves rolling the stone up the hill. Taylor claims that if Sisyphus desires to roll the stone up the hill, then his punishment isn't really punishing him at all. In fact, Taylor claims that in the case where Sisyphus enjoys his punishment he has a meaningful life. Sisyphus's life is meaningful even though he is engaging in an otherwise meaningless and toilsome activity for all eternity.

If subjectivism is true, then it's doubtful that Darrow's life is all that meaningful. While he does enjoy some of the things he does, he often struggles to live for more. He endures extreme physical and emotional pain throughout the trilogy. Overall, it seems that he doesn't really get much joy by living in the way that he does. Thus, it seems that given subjectivism, Darrow's life may not be all that meaningful.

But, is subjectivism correct? Should we really think that all that's required to have a meaningful life is to enjoy the activities that one engages in and live in the manner that one desires? It seems not. Rather than discuss various arguments against subjectivism, let's simply consider a few consequences of accepting this view. These will make it clear that subjectivism is not the way to go.

Brutal killers like Karnus au Bellona or Lilath au Faran, leader of the Boneriders, seem to thoroughly enjoy killing and inflicting suffering on others. They desire to hurt, maim, and kill others. Unfortunately, they're often successful in fulfilling those desires, and they enjoy it when they do. Should we say that their lives are meaningful? What about two other Boneriders: the elder brothers Rath? As Roque au Fabii describes them, "their chief virtue lies in their ability to sin. They're prodigies at it" (*Golden Son*, p. 85). Do they really live meaningful lives? No, it seems not. Perhaps subjectivism is the approach to life endorsed by these killers and various Pixies, but it isn't adequate as an account of life's meaning. In order to have a meaningful life you must live for more than the satisfaction of your own desires.

Objectivism and the Life of Darrow

If subjectivism isn't correct, can Darrow's life be meaningful? Yes, it can. Objectivism allows for Darrow's life to have meaning. Like subjectivism, objectivism is a kind of optimistic naturalism. Accordingly, objectivism also includes the claim that it's unnecessary for God to exist in order for an individual's life to be meaningful. Aside from the shared commitment to this claim, objectivism is very different from subjectivism.

As we've seen, subjectivism is mistaken because it holds that all that matters for meaning in an individual's life is for her to enjoy the activities that she engages in. After all, Karnus, Lilath, and the elder brothers Rath are not exemplars of meaningful lives! Plausibly, we learn from considering these despicable individuals that what's needed in order for an individual's life to be meaningful is that they be engaged in projects that are objectively worthwhile. Rather than simply satisfying your own desires, or even worse hurting and killing innocents, in order to have a meaningful life, you must do things that are good. You have to do things like form loving relationships, search for truth, create beauty, and so on. This makes for a meaningful life.

Unfortunately, being engaged in objectively worthwhile projects isn't enough on its own in order to make a life meaningful. Look at Nero au Augustus. He's about as ruthless and uncaring a Peerless Scarred as any you are likely to meet. He killed his first wife and then sent her head to his father-in-law. He had Darrow's wife hung for singing a song! He's clearly not a good person. And yet, Darrow comes to realize that "There is no morality to him. No goodness. No evil intent when he killed Eo. He believes he is beyond morality. His aspirations are so grand that he has become inhuman in his desperate desire to preserve humanity" (*Golden Son*, p. 430). Preserving humanity is an objectively worthwhile project, and Nero is engaged in that project. He largely devotes his life to this task. Nonetheless, Nero is horrible, and it leaves a bad taste in one's mouth to say that his life is meaningful. What's lacking? Love.

Subjectivism is correct that you must enjoy or love what you do, but it goes wrong in thinking that is all that matters. It would be an equally large mistake to think that all that matters is engaging in worthwhile activities. Both are required for a meaningful life. As philosopher Susan Wolf says,

> one's life is meaningful insofar as one finds oneself loving things worthy of love and able to do something positive about it. A life is meaningful . . . insofar as it is actively and lovingly engaged in projects of worth. (*Meaning in Life and Why It Matters*, p. 35)

This seems right, but what does it tell us about Darrow?

Darrow seems to satisfy both conditions of objectivism. He lives for more. Importantly, his living for more means that he lives for more than himself and his own pleasures. Darrow fights to topple a Society that enslaves and abuses the many for the benefit of the few. He lives for Eo's dream, but more than that, he lives to make a better world for his people and all of the Colors of the Society. Darrow is most assuredly actively engaged in a project of immense worth.

But, is he lovingly engaged in this project? Yes, he is. He starts on this path out of love for his deceased wife, Eo. He continues out of love for his family and friends. Admittedly, there are times when Darrow allows his pride and hatred of the Society to drive him on. This doesn't mean that he's not engaging in this project in a loving fashion though. All it means is that for all of his greatness, Darrow is only human and bound to make mistakes. However, throughout the Rising, Darrow continually grows and acts out of love. This can be seen by contrasting his life with that of his great nemesis, Adrius au Augustus, the Jackal.

Darrow understands the Jackal and expresses his understanding clearly, "Nothing has ever been enough for you, nor will it be. Adrius, you're not trying to prove yourself to your father, to me, to Virginia, to the Sovereign. You're trying to matter to yourself. Because you're broken inside. Because you hate what you are" (*Morning Star*, p. 441). Adrius does what he does out of hatred and self-loathing, whereas Darrow does what he does out of love. Even when he makes mistakes and falls short of the man he could and should be, Darrow continually finds reasons to press on in the love he has for his family, his friends, and his project of changing his world for the better.

Darrow of Lykos, the Reaper of Mars, has a meaningful life because he lives for more—more than himself, more than his pride, more than his own happiness and desires. He lives for others. Perhaps we can learn from Darrow and have meaningful lives of our own whether we are Red or Gold.

Regardless of our struggles, perhaps we can live for more. Per aspera ad astra.

III

To Live or Not to Live in the Society

9
Pierce's Republic

RANDALL M. JENSEN

Society is stratified into Colors. Elite Golds rule like gods on high, while rusty Reds are the backs upon which the Society is built. Every person has a Color, every Color has its place, and the driving principle of the Society is that each person must be kept in his or her place.

This is the world of Pierce Brown's *Red Rising* trilogy. But it's also the world of one of Plato's most well-known dialogues, the *Republic*. Brown has said in an interview that he drew inspiration from Plato's *Republic* for the society depicted in *Red Rising*. Let's see what happens when these two worlds collide.

The Society and the City

Plato's overarching concern in the *Republic* is to define the nature of justice and to show that justice is good for its own sake. His main strategy is utopian: he sketches an account of the ideal City and the Guardians who'll watch over it. The raw material for this class of Guardians is a rare blend of the most desirable intellectual, psychological, and physical traits. Starting at a young age, these Guardians-to-be are put through a comprehensive education and training regimen that would put the Society's Institute to shame. They all live as a community in public housing provided by the

City. They own no property, they also have no family. A secret and carefully controlled lottery is used to make sure that the best of the male and female Guardians mate with one another—Plato's low-tech version of a eugenics program.

The next generation will be raised by all of the Guardians, with no clue about which child is the offspring of which adult. All of this is meant to guarantee that Guardians identify the City's good as their own, making them less likely to be partial and corruptible as most of the Society's Golds seem to be. Plato means for there to be harmony and friendship between the classes in the hierarchy of the City. Each citizen is to be content with his or her lot in life and must gladly affirm the rule of the Guardians who look out for everyone's interests. This City won't be ruled with an iron fist, for it won't need to be.

To help build this kind of ideal society Plato fashions the Myth of the Metals near the end of Book III of the *Republic*. The inhabitants of the City are told that they have all come forth out of the Earth and that a certain type of metal has been mixed into each of their souls: gold into the City's rulers, silver into the Guardians, and iron and bronze into the souls of the craftsmen and workers. This myth Plato calls a Noble Lie.

Although no such birth from the Earth ever occurred, this story is useful for expressing the important truth that different people are suited for different roles in life. It also encourages folks to accept their respective vocational roles as their destiny. Plato depicts this lie as a noble one, because although strictly speaking it is false, as a myth it's meant to produce truth rather than falsehood in the souls of those who hear it.

Plato's City sorts people into three basic categories: Gold, Silver, and Iron or Bronze. The Colorful hierarchy of Pierce's Republic is even more elaborate than Plato's. Golds rule, with Obsidians and Grays serving as their auxiliary forces. "The Whites arbitrate their justice and push their philosophy. Silvers count and manipulate currency and logistics. Yellows study the medicines and sciences. Greens develop technology. Blues navigate the stars. Coppers run the bureaucracy. Every Color has a purpose. Every Color props up the Golds."

Plato's City and Pierce's Society seem to be working from very similar blueprints. However, whereas Plato gives us an idealistic portrait of how his City might be realized in theory, Brown paints us a picture of a decadent Society in conflict. Think of the cruelty and arrogance of the Peerless Scarred and how they regard Pixies as little better than the lowColors they so despise. They're not all that much like Plato's virtuous Guardians. Harmony, a member of the Sons of Ares, tells us that in the Society "Golds structure everything to make their own lives easier." But Plato is emphatic that the City's Guardians are to structure everything for the good of the City as a whole.

Probably, many readers of Plato's *Republic* predict that the City, if ever realized, would turn out to be much like Pierce Brown's Society, in spite of all of Plato's plans and best intentions. Surely anyone who's given the power of a Gold will abuse that power. Does this make Plato naive?

Not so fast. Plato is very clear that he thinks it's unlikely that this City can ever really exist. It's a model designed to help us think about justice and about what we want our lives to be like rather than an action plan for an aspiring dictator. Moreover, later in the *Republic*, Plato tells us that nothing perfect can last, and then, spins a long tale about the degeneration of the City by stages into a vicious tyranny.

So, the apparent distance between the *Republic* and *Red Rising* may not be so great after all. Brown's world is simply drawn more from the end of Plato's lengthy narrative than from the beginning. And neither of these works is primarily political.

The Mine and the Cave

At the beginning of Book VII of the *Republic*, in the famous Allegory of the Cave, Plato once again depicts humanity as beginning life's journey in the darkness under the earth. This time, he says that we're all like prisoners chained to our seats in a Cave, so that all we see are shadows on the wall in front of us. We believe the shifting shadows on the wall to be reality, unaware that we are in chains and there's a whole world outside of the Cave in the light. The only ones to escape this prison—to break the chains, as Darrow would say—are the philosopher kings (and queens), who are the very best of the City's Guardians.

Leto, the protégé of the ArchGovernor of Mars, proclaims that "our imperative to rule exists because we are fit to best guide mankind. We are Plato's philosopher kings. Our cause is order. We provide stability." Of course, not all of the Society's Golds even share this vision of their role, much less live up to it.

Escape from the Cave means both liberation and illumination: knowing the truth about reality is what frees us. Naturally, after their escape, the philosophers would rather remain above ground under the sun, but they'll be compelled by their sense of justice to return to the darkness in order to lead the cave dwellers. They owe a debt to the City for their education and they are the City's best and only hope: only they can see and understand the shadows for what they are.

It's worth pausing here to register that Plato's philosopher king isn't just any old intellectual. I think it's safe to say that none of the professors or self-help gurus you happen to know would measure up to Plato's ambitious vision. What makes these philosopher kings uniquely suited to rule is both that they have the knowledge and the character needed to carry out the task and, somewhat paradoxically, that they'd rather not have the job. Ruling a city properly requires a lot of work for little reward. Plato thinks we ought to be suspicious of the motives of anyone who is enthusiastic about becoming a ruler. What kind of person really wants to become a bureaucrat, after all? And who would want to rule rather than to strive to understand and to love reality itself? The best ruler knows there is more to life than power.

However, Plato isn't optimistic about the prospects of a would-be philosopher ruler. He recognizes that in the world as it is, a philosopher ought to do his best to stay out of trouble—to avoid the fate of his beloved mentor Socrates. Only through some incredible coincidence could a philosopher come to power, or a ruler come to philosophy. What we need for a better society to emerge, then, is something that will probably never happen. No doubt Ares would relate to this.

While the Allegory of the Cave has a particular meaning within Plato's philosophy, it has inspired many people who are intrigued by the big ideas that: A. The world is not as it seems to be; B. Only a few see the world as it truly is, while the many believe a lie; C. To see the world as it truly is requires a kind of conversion, a "turning of the soul," as Plato puts it, from darkness to light; and D. Such a conversion is what makes life worth living, yet most will resist it with all their strength.

Plato's Socrates even acknowledges that the very idea of a philosopher who rules might provoke some in his audience to pick up their swords (or their razors!) with the intent to do him grievous bodily harm, reacting much as the Golds would to the idea that a Red might rule in Brown's world. Anyone who's a sucker for lost causes, whether political or educational or religious or whatever, is likely to be drawn to Plato's Cave Allegory. Like a lot of good allegories, it can be spun into nearly anything.

Darrow's own story is one of ascent out of the darkness and into the light. He quite literally grows up in a cave, or rather a mine. When he first sees the outside world, he doesn't understand what he's looking at. The brightness of the sun blinds him. As he puts it, "my eyes are not used to seeing so far or seeing so much light." Much later, after being betrayed by Roque, when Darrow returns to the mine to visit the garden where he buried Eo, it seems much smaller than he remembers, less colorful, less beautiful.

All this closely mirrors Plato's description of the journey of the philosopher who escapes the Cave—or is somehow forcibly removed from it—and then returns to the darkness. What Plato doesn't imagine is the possibility of a Red becoming a Gold. Not just any prisoner can escape the Cave. To be fair, we should acknowledge that Plato does allow that your

Color isn't solely a matter of your parentage. Reds could give birth to a Gold, and Golds could produce a Red, in the world of Plato's *Republic*. Still, a Red is a Red and a Gold is a Gold.

The Noble Lie of Demokracy

Nero au Augustus, ArchGovernor of Mars, in his welcoming speech to the Institute's newest class of students, speaks proudly of how their ancestors savagely freed themselves "from the shackles of Demokracy, from the Noble Lie—the idea that men are brothers and are created equal." Roque also refers to this Lie in his attempt to convince Romulus to side with Society rather than with the more Demokratic Rising movement.

In Brown's trilogy, the Noble Lie is a thing of the past. It's used by the ascendant aristocratic regime not to support their own societal structure but rather to condemn their disgraced Demokratic forebears. Further, this Demokratic Noble Lie didn't create truth in people's souls but instead led to humanity's ruin, at least according to the Gold regime that is now telling the story. The very expression "Noble Lie" is tainted by Demokracy and is only now used with scornful irony.

Nonetheless, the Society is clearly on board with the idea of a state creating this kind of useful falsehood that functions as a kind of myth. Think of the story told to the lowReds of Mars. The truth the Society actually endorses is that the Reds are the lowest of humans, only suited for the most menial of tasks. But the Society sweetens this bitter pill with a tale of how the Red miners work so bloodydamn hard in such terrible conditions because they're making their planet inhabitable for the rest of humanity. They're heroes suffering for the greater good, or so they think.

In reality the truth is that the planet has already been habitable for seven hundred years as of the time of the Rising and the surface is full of people living in luxury the lowReds can only imagine. So, the Society doesn't really have a problem with the notion of a Noble Lie. It has a problem with Demokracy. Since it's fundamentally misguided,

Demokracy creates the wrong myths to try to teach lies as truth. Augustus's main worry about Darrow is that he's some kind of Demokrat.

In Book VIII of the *Republic*, Plato is also no fan of Demokracy. In a place ruled by Demokracy, people are free to say and do whatever they want and diversity and tolerance are the order of the day. To most of us, this sounds like a good thing, until we realize that for Plato what it implies is that people are likely to take up jobs for which they're in no way suited. And while it's unfortunate if anyone who's working on your behalf is bad at their job, it's a crisis if those who rule the entire City are incompetent. Plato goes on to characterize the person whose soul is Demokratic as someone who lives life in a haphazard way, following the whimsy of his own desires. Sometimes he's a lush. Other times he's a fanatic about his health. One day he's an intellectual, the next he's a practical man. He has no integrity, no real character to call his own. Sadly, this probably reminds all of us of politicians we know.

In this psychological portrait, the freedom Demokracy brings is depicted in an ugly light. Freedom means no order, no discipline, no competence, no direction. Plato would understand why Darrow says, "I see why Demokracy is illegal. First comes yelling. Frustration. Indecision. Disagreements. Ideas . . ." Any carefully constructed and optimally functioning regime may well collapse if Demokracy is allowed to spread. Inefficiency at best and outright civil war at worst, this is what worries the elite Golds of the Society.

Plato has a point. When we give people freedom, whether in society in general, or in a classroom, or in one of the Houses of the Institute, or in a cell of the Sons of Ares, things don't always run smoothly. There's an understandable reason why most modern democracies aren't pure democracies. We don't always want what's good for us. We frequently don't realize where our strengths and weaknesses lie. We often don't know what we're talking about, yet that doesn't stop us from talking—or acting. We make rash, uninformed, and foolish decisions. Sometimes chaos ensues!

Plato reminds us that those who want to defend freedom ought to reckon with its bad consequences as well as its good ones. However, even for Plato there is something worse than a Demokrat: a Tyrant. If Plato's ideal City is out of reach, perhaps we're caught in the struggle between Demokracy and Tyranny.

Red and Gold

Plato's *Republic* might be seen as the story of the Rising of the Gold philosopher kings in a world ruled by the powers of the marketplace and the courtrooms and the battlefield. As we've seen, Plato realizes it will take some kind of miracle for this to happen. Escape from the Cave is difficult.

The *Republic* is also an aristocratic story told from the top looking down. Socrates and the people he converses with imagine themselves as the founders of the City and spend most of their time thinking about those who will shape society. Those who rule over the city are themselves ruled by the best part of their souls, reason reigning over the spirited part of the soul and the appetites.

But what about the City's laborers, the Platonic equivalent of the Society's lowReds? We don't hear very much about them. Near the end of the dialogue, Socrates remarks that because their own reason is too weak, menial workers and slaves aren't capable of ruling themselves. Thus, it's best for them to be ruled by the reason of the rulers. In Plato's City, what's important about the masses is that they're kept in their place and content to be governed by their betters. We can easily imagine one of the Society's elitist Golds making this argument, although Plato will insist that it really is for the good of the ruled and not merely for the convenience of the rulers. Someone like Roque or Augustus might say this, too, but I doubt we'd buy it any more than Ares would.

Brown's story, obviously, is about the Rising of the Reds. Through Darrow's eyes we see the Society from the very bottom up. And, as Darrow rises, as the Red Helldiver of Lykos becomes the Gold Primus of House Mars and then eventually defeats Roque's fleet and dethrones and kills the Sovereign, we see a living refutation of the Society's belief that Color determines your destiny. Of course, Darrow doesn't and couldn't do all this alone. His Rising also shows that friendship and loyalty can defeat fear and servitude. The Reaper couldn't have won without Sevro and the Howlers, without Ragnar, without Mustang, without Dancer, without Mickey, without the help of many, many others. Even Cassius eventually returns to his side. In the end, freedom and real community triumph over tyranny.

Darrow's central message, his gospel, if you will, is that we get to choose who we are, what Color we are. In fact, as Darrow shows by removing his Sigils, perhaps there really aren't any Colors. The Color system is a tool of the Society, not an accurate picture of human nature.

As the Reaper's first Iron Rain begins, he thinks to himself, "Man wasn't born to be any Color. Our rulers decided to relegate us to Colors. And they were wrong." Near the end of the Rising, as the final space battle begins, he pronounces to his fleet that, "We are not Red, not Blue or Gold or Gray or Obsidian. We are humanity. We are the tide. And today we reclaim the lives that have been stolen from us." When he's trying to convince Victra to join him, he tells her, "I truly believe we choose who we want to be in this life. It isn't preordained."

As he reveals his true history to Ragnar Volarus, the great Stained Obsidian who'll become his close companion and the Shield of Tinos, he says that, "We have languished in darkness. But there will come a day when we walk in the light . . . It will come when brave hearts rise and choose to break the chains, to live for more. You must choose for yourself." After he finally bares his soul to Mustang, he begs her to see the truth that "You aren't Gold. We aren't Red. We're people, Mustang. Each of us can change. Each of us can be what we like."

This is in sharp contrast to the Society's message that our lot in life is settled by our birth and our native abilities. In the Sovereign's speech she praises the Society's commitment to duty and "the immortality of the human race on principles of order and prosperity." Octavia affirms the Hierarchy of

Color. To believe that we can choose our Color is to risk falling into darkness. Plato would agree with her words, it seems, even if like us he'd question her sincerity. Where we're placed in society is crucial to our flourishing, both individually and corporately. And when so much is at stake, we simply can't afford to trust the masses.

As readers of the *Red Rising* trilogy, we travel with Darrow on his journey. We share his grief and his anger and his hope. We resonate with his message and his mission. We want to believe that a Red can rise. And yet, we must ask, can just any Red become the Reaper? In fact, most Reds can't even be a Helldiver. Darrow has the nerve, the mental acuity, the dexterity, and the skill to do this most difficult of jobs. Even before his dramatic Carving and training, Darrow isn't just anybody. Uncle Narol and the Sons of Ares saw something in him.

Aren't there significant limits on what any of us can choose to be? Not just anyone can be the Reaper or the Jackal. Not just anyone can be anything. Surely some can't function as a Green or a Blue, even if they want to do so. Some Reds can't be Golds and some Golds can't be Reds, at least not without the services of someone like Mickey who can seemingly reshape anyone into anything. That's no small point, either. In a world where such things are possible, what does it mean to give everyone an equal opportunity in life?

In our own world, some of us can't sing, even though we dream of a musical career. And some of us are just no good at math and science, and so we have to forget about the idea of becoming a doctor. And we have no miracle worker to give us some kind of genetic upgrade. So what do we make of Darrow's belief that we get to choose who we become? Is it just a bit of rhetorical hyperbole?

It seems to me that his real point is not that we somehow get to create ourselves out of nothing, but rather that we shouldn't be constrained by society's limits or its expectations of us. Sure, if I can't do the math, then I can't be a Blue engineer. But if society tells me I can't be an engineer because I don't fit some social stereotype or because people of my sort can't get an education, then I ought to break the chains.

112

I think we have to be honest about two more clarifications of the nature of Darrow's gospel. We've already seen that Darrow's success doesn't depend only on his own choices and his own efforts. Many other people pave the way for him and come alongside him. Now, we should notice the extent to which his victories depend on luck. At any number of points along the way, his mission could've failed if things had gone just a bit differently.

So, you can choose who you want to be in life, within limits—if you're lucky and if you've got an awful lot of help. That doesn't play well in a rousing speech, but it's closer to the truth. Second, there's no guarantee that you'll succeed in the project of becoming whoever you want to be. What Darrow offers you is the chance to try—and sometimes to fail. Arguably, that's what Demokracy has to offer, too: the freedom to lose your way as well as to chart your own course.

Morning Star

In the third story of the trilogy, Darrow is given yet another name. Not only is he the Reaper, a bringer of death, he is also the Morning Star, a source of hope and light. As he says to Sevro after the death of Ragnar, "You and I keep looking for light in the darkness, expecting it to appear. But it already has. We're it, boyo. Broken and cracked and stupid as we are, we're the light, and we're spreading."

Whereas in Plato's *Republic* the source of illumination is a realm of transcendent Forms, Beauty and Justice and Goodness, here in the world of *Red Rising* the light comes from people. And not from their perfection, but from their love and guts and determination in spite of their many flaws. It's fitting that the trilogy closes not with any kind of political or philosophical statement, but with Darrow's intent to remember and retell the story of "the rage of Ares, the strength of Ragnar, the honor of Cassius, the love of Sevro, the loyalty of Victra, and the dream of Eo, the girl who inspired me to live for more."

10
Virtue Rising

DARCI DOLL

When Darrow enlisted with the Sons of Ares, he only knew that it would give him a chance to fulfill Eo's dream of breaking the chains. He didn't fully understand what Eo meant, nor why this is something for which she was willing to die. He only knew he would be the tool to carry out her dying request.

As he was brought in with the Sons, he learned that even Eo couldn't have understood the root of the chains. He would have to painfully learn the extent to which the Society was corrupt and deceptive; a lesson outside of Eo's imagination. She knew there was an injustice in how the (low)Reds were living, but the depths of the duplicity were more than any one, independent of Color, could have fathomed.

The ways in which the Society deceived and exploited the different Colors were outlined in *Red Rising, Golden Son,* and *Morning Star.* What wasn't discussed was the intellectual vacuum revealed by the rebellion. Intellectual oppression is utilized to secure the Society and the rule of the Golds. As this intellectual oppression is lifted, we see an intellectual revolution begin to take shape.

Golden Intellectual Reformation

The Rising of the Sons revealed that each level of the Society, apart from the highest of the Golds, was denied true freedom of education. The Society was intentionally built on a series of "noble" lies, deprivation of education, and selected information. The Golds who orchestrated this intellectual deficit justified it by arguing that it was in the best interest of the individual citizens and the Society as a whole.

These Golds argued that the lower Colors were incapable of higher-order understanding, or that ignorance was bliss for them. Therefore, it was claimed to be noble for the Golds to be selective with what the various Colors were able to learn and know. They also argued that the weight of the knowledge and the responsibility of ruling the Society was a burden Golds bore for the greater good of all of the Colors. When the Sons disrupted the Golds' rule of the Society, citizens became aware of the lies, their imposed ignorance, and the amount of information available. Based on what we see in the trilogy, this uncovering of ignorance brought about by the Rising created an Intellectual Reformation.

In the Intellectual Reformation, individuals learned the degrees to which they had been denied knowledge about the history of the Society, the current structure of the Society, their roles in the Society, as well as basic educational diversity. It was revealed that access to history, philosophy, science, mathematics, even the ability to read and write, was dictated by what the Society felt was appropriate for each Color—their station and function in life.

With the dissemination of this material, it also became clear that Golds were incorrect—Color doesn't dictate intellectual or educational potential. Darrow is a good example of one who exceeded the assumed fate of his Color. Despite being born a lowRed, with the help of mentors, educators, and other supplements, he was able to learn to read and understand complex texts and demonstrate knowledge so well that the Board of Quality Control suspected him of cheating on various tests of Gold aptitude.

A lowRed out-performed the best of the Golds. You might complain that Darrow's abilities are just the result of Mickey's carving. True, but Darrow isn't our only example, boyo! In *Golden Son*, Orion xe Aquarii is a Blue who, with no special carving, is able to think logically and intuitively enough to help the *Pax* escape. Ragnar and Sefi are also good examples of characters thinking outside of their "pre-determined" Color to excel at tasks otherwise deemed impossible. The Intellectual Reformation, then, wasn't just about the access to information; it was also an awakening to the fact that intellectual potential isn't determined by Color.

Apologia

A city comes to be because none of us is self-sufficient, but we all need many things.

—PLATO's *Republic,* Book II, line 369b

The justification of the Society's hierarchy appears many millennia ago. In the fourth century B.C.E. (following the old Earth timeline), a Greek Philosopher called Plato wrote the *Republic*, consisting of ten books. Despite it being a historical Earth text, Plato's ideal society in the *Republic* claims that the elite of society should take a paternalistic role over its less-capable members. In return for this responsibility, the Philosopher Kings (as Plato calls them, who are analogous to the Society's Peerless Scarred) are endowed with what may appear to be more freedoms and luxuries. The burden they carry, however, is that they are responsible for ensuring that everyone stays in their designated roles. Heavy is the heart of the rulers of Society.

Plato's original goal was to discuss individual human goods, such as justice and happiness. Throughout the development of the books of the *Republic*, though, Plato's dialectical discourse moved from the discussion of a Good person to the analogy of a Good city; the suggestion was that a Good person would be ordered the same as a Good city. Therefore, if we can identify the ideal city, we'd have the framework upon which to identify the ideal person.

After the philosophical consideration of some basic features of cities, it's proposed that the ideal city will be one where each member contributes to the wellbeing of the society as a whole. It was also decided that there would essentially be three levels of society: those who produce, those who enforce, and those who rule. Those who produce, Plato asserted, would have the most basic skills, abilities, and educational capacities. These individuals are workers who produce the goods and services other members of society need in order to survive. In the Society, these are the lowColors. The ones whose labor fulfills the essential needs of all of the members of Society; for example, the lowReds who mine the helium-3, who aren't taught to read or write, who have only the essential educational experiences that allow them to keep producing.

A second group in Plato's society, those who enforce the laws and ensure the safety of the society and its constituents, are known as *auxiliaries*. Auxiliaries include those who are more adept with respect to physical and militaristic strengths and skills. These individuals maintain the order that allows society to flourish. In the Society, these are the Greys and Obsidians. Their educational training is limited to the traits needed to enforce the laws and maintain social order; they are bred for strength and physical superiority.

As we see with Ragnar, education beyond physical development and law enforcement is limited to myths—Noble Lies—that teach them to fear stepping out of their place. They're taught that they are ruled by Gods, and that independent thinking, questioning authority, and so on, are vices to be avoided and feared.

In both Plato's *Republic* and the Society, these "lower" groups are taught that obedience is the highest virtue. They dedicate their lives to the good of the Society but are never endowed with knowledge of the role they play. Unquestioning obedience and loyalty to the Society is all these groups are entitled to. So, they are basically slaves to society, though that's not what they're told. Realizing, they'll be happier believing they're free, Reds are given the Noble Lie that they're the most important Color, since it's they who will save humanity.

The final group in Plato's city are the rulers, or guardians. These will be the people of the best breeding, the best genes, but more importantly, the best intellectual abilities. These are the ones who can truly understand philosophy, the Good, what's best for the society, and how to rule and protect those below them.

Plato believed the guardians deserved the best intellectual and physical education. The cost of their superior status is the burden of being responsible for the wellbeing of all levels of society; they have to suffer the knowledge of all of the necessary sacrifices needed to make the city survive. Unlike the other members of society, these rulers know the sacrifices that are made to make the society function—they know the truth.

The Society's Golds, or at least the premier Golds—the Peerless Scarred, are very similar to Plato's guardians. Prior to Darrow's year at the Institute, the ArchGovenor Augustus told the Golds that men are not equal, "A Red can no more command a starship than a Green can serve as a Doctor!"

The Golds are the best of humanity, but to become the best of the Golds, the Peerless Scarred, they must sacrifice. They have to learn, in the tests of the Institute, the costs of ruling. They have to learn how to function, how to make sacrifices for the greater good, to learn the importance of sustaining and protecting the stability of the Colors. After all, the wellbeing of every citizen of the Society depends upon it.

Having the privilege of learning Plato, the Golds know that in order to secure the order of the Society, it's important to keep each level in their role. This means that they have to ensure that the lower Colors don't try to step outside of their station. Threats of democracy, like rebellion (such as that of the Sons of Ares), endanger every member of Society.

Insights of Oversight

As a result of the Sons' rebellion, the intellectual vacuum became filled. All of the Colors gained access to information reserved for Golds, and materials hidden by Golds became available.

While investigating other historical Earth texts, a contemporary of Plato's was discovered—Aristotle. It seems that

Plato's ideal society was lacking. In particular, Aristotle argued that human potential can only be realized in the right environment, with the right instruction, and with the use of their rational faculties. For Aristotle, people aren't born good or bad, they're made good or bad. Individuals may have some innate potential, but it can only be achieved when given the opportunity to develop. Therefore, the Platonic/Societal emphasis on location of birth/Color is an unsuitable way to determine and maximize an individual's potential.

Darrow, or Reaper, is just one example of an individual born as a Red who, when given the right circumstances, demonstrated having a quality comparable, or even superior, to the Golds. The same is true for the others mentioned above.

Aristotle might say that the tales of these "low" Colors, who become Gold-like, demonstrate an ability to find the golden mean necessary for successful, harmonious leadership and individual flourishing. Darrow is able to demonstrate that obedience isn't the ultimate virtue. By breaking away from the assumption that Color of birth determines potential, Darrow is able to excel in all of the tests presented to the Golds.

Darrow's one of the few who can understand the paradigm of the Society, the limitations of the paradigm, and how to change the paradigm for the better. It's not just that he's been carved to be better, but his inner-character helps him make wise and right decisions. He's able to understand the Society so well that he uses the Society to undermine itself. In undermining the Society it's shown that the truly ideal society is one where people are encouraged to cultivate their strengths and maximize their potential. In an ideal society people are subsequently assigned social roles based on their demonstrated abilities.

Aristotle said, "Therefore only an utterly senseless person can fail to know that our characters are the result of our conduct." He believed that the character, or quality, of a person is dependent upon the education, the environment, and the actions of that individual. Darrow, for example, was able to excel at the colony of Lykos because he was able to understand the environment, and he had the wisdom of when to take risks and when to play it safe. His experiences shaped him and made him capable of these two features of his character. When he did well as a Helldiver, he reinforced and habituated those character traits. When he did poorly, he learned from his mistakes and learned how to avoid such failures in the future. This awareness, ability, and commitment to action is likely what led Eo to see that Darrow could be more than a mere Red. She saw that he could be a tool of the great social change, in which she so strongly believed. She saw he could learn, grow, and lead people.

When made into a Gold, Darrow maintained and enhanced these abilities. He adapted to his environment, he learned everything he could, and relied on what Aristotle would call "practical wisdom" to help him identify what virtuous actions were "best" in each situation. Like Aristotle, Darrow didn't do what was best, in the sense of what would get him material gains, but instead, he did what was best in the sense of being the best version of himself possible.

Throughout his mission, we see that Darrow isn't always perfect. He often makes mistakes, some of which are catastrophic, for example his interactions with Titus and Cassius. His strength is that he doesn't allow these mistakes to define him. He reassesses his decisions, the type of person his actions are turning him into (his character), and questions whether his new character is consistent with Eo's dream.

When Eo asked Darrow to break the chains, neither she nor Darrow knew what it'd take to break the chains and improve the society. Darrow was only able to figure out the best way to improve the Society by constantly testing himself, reflecting, and growing from his experiences. In this way, he lived the life of courageous flourishing condoned by Aristotle. The practical wisdom and habituation of character is what allowed Darrow to break the chains despite the significant obstacles created by the Society.

The Real Rising

Aristotle argued that the ideal friendships and types of rule are those that are focused on a sincere desire for the good of each other. Aristotle criticized institutions like those in Plato's *Republic*, which means he wouldn't be a fan of the Society either. These political organizations are focused only on utility. This means that the relationship (whether it's friendship or political order) will fail as soon as its usefulness has been exhausted. In the Society, we see that non-useful members are expendable. Political agreements fall apart when the usefulness of the agreements expire, which leads to moons being eradicated with nuclear weapons.

In the Society fidelity, friendships, and loyalty are all subject to expiration, usually in a very gruesome way. We see this with people like Antonia. Her loyalty, dedication, and resources were only devoted to those that she felt were beneficial, and vice versa. Once she lost her usefulness to the Sovereign and the Jackal, after abandoning Roque during the Battle of the Jovian moons, she was dispassionately executed.

Darrow and Mustang were more than just friends of utility. They became friends and joined others by establishing respect, balance, and consideration for the wellbeing of those they partnered with and ruled. By developing friendships based on these principles, they implemented Aristotle's ideal. In the Institute they were able to secure the true loyalty of the Oathbreakers and their "slaves" by leading with justice. They established the importance of the success of each individual as essential to the whole, like Mustang's example of the hand, and how the reciprocal sincere concern for the individual is what made the whole unit possible.

Because they led with virtue and justice, Darrow and Mustang were able to get people to fight alongside them, even after Darrow's true Red Color was revealed. They were able to demonstrate that merit comes from conviction, action, and reasoning, not Color. It is from this philosophical point of view that they're able to get the loyalty of other Colors as well. Their willingness to let Ragnar, Orion, and Sefi be independent, free individuals, to demonstrate their merit uninhibited by Color, allowed Ragnar, Orion, and Sefi to help maximize the effectiveness of their army. When each individual is allowed to develop and cultivate their full potential, everyone is better off.

Unlike what the Society orchestrated, Mustang and Darrow are rebuilding a civilization focused on valuing all individuals and letting them maximize their potential. Sure, what Augustus said is right: some Reds can man a starship, Greens can be doctors, Golds can be monsters. However, his claim that allowing them to do such things will disrupt the order of the Society isn't a good enough reason to justify the existence of the oppressive Society. As *Red Rising* shows, if you rule with virtuous character, and empower individuals, great things can happen.

The things preventing the various low Colors from performing jobs outside of their Gold restricted parameters wasn't an innate biological inability; it was selective deprivation of options and information. Once individuals were told they weren't bound by the chains of their Colors, we began to see how great they could be. A strong case for Aristotle's theory, indeed.

Gorydamn Equality

A couple of millennia after Aristotle (still many millennia prior to the rise of the Society) a new approach to philosophy emerged; one that indirectly maintained Aristotle's idea of potential and opportunity. This new wave, however, showed that the concepts weren't being applied equally to men and women. In fact, some of these nineteenth- and twentieth-century (by the Earth timeline) individuals argued that women and certain humans of color were being intentionally kept from achieving their potential. Like Reds, they were being denied education and individual freedom. They were at best considered "lower" citizens, and at worst slaves.

The limitation of women and people of color, as a form of oppression, is clearly seen throughout *Red Rising*, but especially in the lowReds. The mining Reds are denied the most freedoms, and their potential for growth is the most limited. This includes a division of labor based on their color and their sex. The only saving grace of the other Colors is that the other Colors have an extension of Aristotle's view of potential and excellence. Though each color is limited in its own way, at least within each Color, women are seen as just as capable as men when it comes to fulfilling tasks (and in some instances, better). So, within each Color, we at least get the insight that excellence is a result of opportunity and character; not the circumstances of birth.

As we evaluate the moral merit of the revolution we can keep in mind that the tales of *Red Rising*, *Golden Son*, and *Morning Star* have shown us that only when all individuals, including women, are in an environment that allows them to flourish and maximize their potential will society finally be capable of maximizing its own potential.

It is yet to be determined the type of society that will *rise* from Mustang and Darrow's revolution. However, their past experiences show their character dictates it will be better than Plato's or the Society's, and quite possibly better than Aristotle's ideal. These two have led a revolution of understanding that will only flourish as a society if we give each individual the opportunity to excel and habituate good character.

11
Beautiful Colors and Unjust Societies

DEVON BRICKHOUSE-BRYSON

Works of science fiction often present us with an imagined society. With the advent of space travel, genetic modification, or cybernetics, the stories go, human societies change dramatically. These visions of the future are not universally grim. The Federation of *Star Trek* has virtuous cosmopolitan features.

But a subset of science fiction takes a less rosy view. Coming to fruition with works like *Brave New World, Animal Farm, Nineteen Eighty-Four*, and *Fahrenheit 451,* this genre is known as *dystopian* literature. *Red Rising* is often said by commentators to fit into this category. These works, and the many others like them, portray societies that are dismal, unjust, and ugly. Often they use this dark vision of the future to instruct us about our present moral situation.

Utopian or dystopian imaginings have a long pedigree in philosophy as well. The term itself—"utopia"—was coined by Thomas More, an English political philosopher from the sixteenth century, who wrote a philosophical work of fiction simply called *Utopia.* In it he imagines an ideal isolated republic reminiscent of a monastic order with complicated rules for voting. And long before that, Plato, in fourth-century B.C.E. Athens, argued for a particular view of justice by imagining an ideal society in his dialogue *Republic.*

Plato's ideal society is organized into several distinct castes, and he argues that justice consists in each of these castes contributing in their particular way to the unity and proper functioning of the society. Even when a complete society isn't explicitly envisioned, political philosophy often relies upon idealizing abstractions or illustrates arguments by means of imagined societies. The so-called "state of nature" is a device used by many Enlightenment political philosophers to motivate their particular views about the ideal society.

To describe a society as "utopian" means that it's a perfect or ideal society. But perfection is a tricky concept. To say that something is perfect means roughly that it possesses some good property to a maximal degree. But this means that something can be perfect in one respect, and yet not perfect in another respect. For example, a Blue pilot can have perfect eyesight and yet not perfect aim: She can score perfectly on one metric and yet not perfectly on another metric.

So, when something has more than one property that makes it good, saying it's "perfect" is ambiguous—it has more than one meaning. We could mean either that it possesses *one* good property to a maximal degree or that it possesses *another* good property to a maximal degree. We would, of course, ultimately want it to possess *all* good properties to a maximal degree: to be perfectly perfect, as it were. But if we're to be clear in our thinking about perfection, we must carefully distinguish the various ways in which a thing can be perfect.

So when we say that a utopian society is a perfect society, which perfections do we have in mind? That is, what are the properties that a society should have that a perfect society would have to a maximal degree? The first thing that comes to mind is that a utopian society should be perfectly *just*. From the range of examples I gave above, this is the main property that science-fiction authors and philosophers have in mind when imaging their societies.

Plato and More are explicitly concerned with justice when constructing their ideal societies, and the dystopias of Huxley, Orwell, and Bradbury are marked by extreme injustice. The Society of *Red Rising*, with its ruthless oppression of the Reds and Pinks in particular, is no exception. The systematic, breathtaking cruelty of the Golds dooms their Society to utter injustice. In this way, the Society is unquestionably dystopian.

But justice isn't the only good property that a society can or should possess. Indeed, there are many examples of utopias from literature that are perfect with respect to some other good besides justice. Consider the cases of Hobbiton, Rivendell, or Lothlórien from Tolkien's *The Lord of the Rings*. These are all good candidates for utopias: they are perfect or ideal societies. But they aren't particularly concerned with justice. We're never shown the hobbits' or elves' systems of government or labor. It's not as though these societies are unjust; it's just that they aren't particularly concerned with justice or that their justice is a mere background assumption. If anything, they are *beyond* justice. In what respect are they perfect societies then, if not with respect to justice? I suggest that they are perfectly *beautiful* societies.

Beauty is, *all else being equal*, a good property for a thing to have. And societies can possess beauty. So, a perfectly beautiful society is properly described as a utopia. But this is different from saying that the society in question is a utopia *in the sense of being perfectly just*. There are plausibly other good properties that a society should have, besides justice and beauty. These other good properties would generate senses of "utopia" of their own. But here we're looking at just societies and beautiful societies, both utopias in their own way. The Society of *Red Rising* is a good case for thinking through this contrast.

Razors and Abstract Objects

So, what do we mean when we say that a society is beautiful? That is, what would make a society beautiful?

At first, we might look to a society's *material culture* in judging the beauty of that society. For instance, we can look at a society's architecture and craftsmanship—its gravBoots, its razors, its clawDrills, its Carvings, and so on. The reasoning might go: When the objects of a society's material culture are, on aggregate, sufficiently beautiful, then that society is beautiful.

In a similar way, we might look to the beauty of a society's *individual members* in judging the beauty of that society. (Antonia certainly thinks she contributes to the beauty of the Society!) Again, the reasoning might go: When the individual members of a society are, on aggregate, sufficiently beautiful, then that society is beautiful.

When I talk about judging things to be beautiful, you might immediately think: "But beauty is merely in the eye of the beholder." It's difficult to articulate what this adage precisely means. But you might take it to mean: "Judgments of beauty are utterly relative to individual persons, such that there's no adjudicating between competing judgments of beauty." This view is roundly rejected throughout the history of philosophizing about beauty. Nor is this view backed by common sense: There's widespread agreement that some artworks are more beautiful than others, some natural landscapes are more worthy of preservation than others because of their beauty.

There *are* difficult questions about the status of judgments of beauty: Are they principled or unprincipled? Is beauty mind-dependent or not? Is beauty *located*, as it were, in the world or in us? Answering these questions is the task of a theory of beauty. But answering these questions one way or the other does not entail that judgments of beauty are utterly relative in the way claimed above. Note also that there are analogous questions about judgments of right and wrong, but we're not thus driven to relativism about morality. It's not my purpose here to develop a theory of beauty, nor will I take up any of these questions. I'm merely assuming that *some* of our judgments of beauty are genuine, and we can thus speak fruitfully of judgments of beauty in general.

The beauty of a society's material culture and of individual human persons is important and worth thinking carefully about. The beauty of a material culture or a collection of persons *might* be what we're referring to when we make the judgment, "That society is beautiful." When we make such a judgment we may be merely speaking in shorthand: our judgment is *actually* about the society in question's material culture or its individual members. But these can't be the core meaning of the notion of a "beautiful society." This is because, roughly speaking, societies are distinct from their material culture and their individual members. That is, they're not merely reducible to their material culture or their individual members.

Consider the following analogy: We often evaluate particular pieces of music as beautiful. For example, we might assert, "Roque's favorite opera, *Tristan and Isolde*, is beautiful." What do we mean by this? We don't, of course, mean that the individual notes of the opera are each beautiful. Nor do we mean what would be even stranger: that the instruments that are used in a given performance of the opera are beautiful or that the paper on which the opera is written is beautiful. We mean that the opera *itself* is beautiful.

All those things—the notes, the instruments, the score— are necessary for the performance of the opera, but the opera is not reducible to those things. Instead, the opera is an *abstract object*: an object that exists, but does not physically exist at any particular place or time. Rather than a mere aggregation of sounds—notes—or a collection of the tools of performance—instruments and scores—the opera is a *system* of musical objects in a certain arrangement. It is *that* abstract object that we're evaluating as beautiful when we say, "*Tristan and Isolde* is beautiful."

Pieces of music aren't the only abstract objects: equations—*systems* of mathematical objects—are a familiar type of abstract objects. Theories—*systems* of explanation—are another example of abstract objects. (Notably, both equations and theories are arguably properly evaluable in terms of beauty, but that's a subject for another time.) Societies are another type of abstract object. A piece of music is an abstract object that is not reducible to the notes, instruments, and scores that instantiate a particular performance of it.

Analogously, a society is an abstract object that isn't reducible to its individual members or to its material culture.

Instead, a society is a *system* of persons ordered into a community; such a system is an abstract object. Individual members and material culture are necessary to instantiate the society at any given place and time, but this does not mean that the society is reducible to them. So, when we say, "That society is beautiful," we are, if we're speaking precisely, evaluating the society *itself*, which is an abstract object, not the society's material culture or its individual members.

Carving Through the History of Beauty

We clarified our question—What makes a society, *conceived as an abstract object, a system of persons*, beautiful?—but are no closer to answering it. What could make an abstract object beautiful? Philosophers rarely give formal definitions of the concept of beauty (it's one of our most difficult concepts to pin down). But there's a longstanding tradition in philosophy of thinking of beauty in terms of *harmoniousness*—for an object to be beautiful is for it to exhibit harmoniousness. We can in turn roughly define 'harmoniousness' as consisting of *an appropriate or coherent ordering of an object's parts*.

For example, a terraformed landscape is harmonious if the various colors, shapes, and grounds that compose the landscape are ordered so as to create a unified effect. Or, another example, Roque's poetry is harmonious if the language, rhythm, and themes come together to achieve a unified effect. Thinking of beauty in this way has a long pedigree in the history of philosophy, notably in Aristotle, Aquinas, and Francis Hutcheson.

This definition of beauty also brings us back to Plato. With the definition of beauty as the unified ordering of parts, we can see that Plato's society in his *Republic* looks suspiciously as if it is meant to instantiate this definition. Plato's ideal society as imagined in *Republic* is divided into distinct castes. These are the various parts that compose that society. Remember that a society is a system of persons ordered into a community. Plato imagines these castes as each contributing, in the way appropriate to their particular strengths, to the unity and the proper functioning of the whole society. Thus, on the definition of beauty as harmoniousness—the ordering of parts into a unified whole—Plato's imagined society in *Republic* is a beautiful society.

Plato doesn't explicitly develop his imagined society to fit a definition of beauty. His explicit goal is to imagine a society that is *just*, and this should be distinguished from a society's beauty. But the definition of justice that Plato argues for using his imagined society is very similar to the definition of beauty that we've been developing here! Nevertheless, theories of justice developed since Plato have diverged significantly from Plato's definition. At the very least we shouldn't assume that beauty and justice always coincide and we should thus work to keep the conceptual distinction clear.

We now have a plausible definition of beauty, drawn from a major tradition of philosophical thinking about beauty. This definition isn't without its problems or its detractors, nor is it the only definition of beauty on offer in the history of philosophy or in contemporary philosophy. But it is a helpful starting point for thinking about beauty and about the beauty of societies in particular. We also see how this definition is meant to apply to various objects, including Plato's imagined society. But the Society of *Red Rising* provides a more fully imagined example that helps us think through this definition of the beauty of societies and how such beauty might diverge from the justice of societies.

Are the Colors Beautiful?

If I asked you, "Is the Society of *Red Rising* beautiful?" you might well react with horror. The very suggestion that the Society—with the brutal labor system the Reds are subjected to; the objectification the Pinks are subjected to; the very limited freedoms awarded to the Browns, Grays, Blues, Greens, Yellows, and other castes; the systematic lies that are told to the Reds and the Obsidians; and the brutality that the Golds display to even their own—could be beautiful might sound perverse.

But let's think about the Society in terms of the definition of beauty developed above. If beauty is the ordering of the parts of an object into a unified whole, then the Society straightforwardly satisfies this definition.

The Society is composed of several distinct castes: The Reds are the laborers, the Pinks are the—ahem—entertainers, the Obsidians are the warriors, the Browns are the servants, the Grays are the police, the Oranges are the mechanics, the Violets are the artists, the Greens are the technicians, the Yellows are the doctors, the Blues are the pilots, the Coppers are the bureaucrats, the Whites are the priests, the Silvers are the businessmen, and the Golds are the rulers.

Not only are the members of these castes firmly educated into their particular roles, we're led to believe (although it may be Gold propaganda) that the castes are *teleologically* distinct. To say that the castes are teleologically distinct means that they have different purposes, they're biologically and mentally suited to their particular roles. Each of the roles that one of the Colors fills is an important part of a unified and well-functioning society. If the distinct castes work together to achieve such a unified and well-functioning society, then that looks like an instance of harmoniousness. The Colors of the Society are the distinct parts of the Society that together achieve a unity, just like the beauty of a well-functioning clock.

Now, there are a couple of points to think carefully about. First, the harmoniousness of the society that I sketched above may be illusory or only surface-deep. If the castes are *not* teleologically distinct (and the claim that they're teleologically distinct is merely Gold propaganda) such that they are *not* biologically and mentally suited to their particular roles, then there's no reason to think that dividing society into rigid castes contributes to the unity and proper functioning of society. The diversity of such arbitrary castes would *not* contribute to the unity of the society, and thus would not fulfill our definition of beauty.

Indeed, such an arbitrary distinction would perhaps run directly *counter* to our definition of beauty. It would introduce varieties that *undermine* the unity of the whole. Thus, on this reading, the Society *seems* beautiful, but penetrating the lies of the Golds shows that the Society isn't beautiful. Indeed, this might show that it's particularly ugly: it introduces varieties that undermine the unity of the whole and hence is a cacophony, not a symphony.

Second, arguing that the Society is beautiful isn't a defense of the *justice* of the Society. Contrary to Plato's insistence that justice consists in each part fulfilling its appropriate role, the Society provides a perfect case for demonstrating how such a situation could still be radically unjust. That is, we might precisely use the Society to argue that Plato's definition of justice is inadequate or to argue that he is better understood as developing an account of the beauty of societies.

The Society's harmoniousness may be illusory, as we discussed above. If this is so, then not only will it not be a beautiful society, but it will not be a counterexample to Plato's account of justice! This is because the appearance that it satisfies Plato's definition of justice would be illusory, just as the appearance that it satisfies our definition of beauty would be illusory. Penetrating the lies of the Golds would show *both* its beauty and its Platonic justice to be illusory.

But we also don't want to assume that Plato is right that beauty and justice must go together. If we did conclude that the Society is beautiful, for the reasons given above, then this should not compel us to think that it's thereby just. It's a perfectly coherent position to claim that the Society is indeed beautiful, but radically unjust. At the very least, we need to think more about the relationship between beauty and justice: when and how they can come apart.

Dystopian and Utopian

This brings us back to the question of utopias. Is the Society of *Red Rising* dystopian? I have never questioned that the Society is radically unjust and thus radically dystopian *with respect to justice*. But we've found that it may not be dystopian *with respect to beauty*. Indeed, if harmoniousness is the correct account of beauty, and the Society does genuinely satisfy that definition, then the Society may be *utopian* with respect to beauty. That is, it might be a particularly good instance of harmoniousness and thus the Society would be an object of great (and terrible) beauty. This would mean that the Society is both dystopian *and* utopian in importantly different respects. Such a conclusion is strange, but it's a good example of the interesting conclusions that clear and careful thinking can reach.

I haven't meant here to definitively weigh in on the question of whether the Society is beautiful or ugly or on whether it's utopian with respect to beauty or not. The purpose of going through this line of thought is to help us think clearer about what it means for a society to be beautiful and to think carefully about how that relates to a society's justice. Perhaps Plato is right that the beauty and justice of a society go hand-in-hand. Then the deep injustice of the Society indicates deep ugliness as well, despite the seeming satisfaction of a plausible definition of beauty. On the other hand, perhaps the Society provides us a case for showing just how much the beauty and justice of a society can *diverge*.

The question of whether the Society is beautiful or not turns on whether the Colors are *genuinely* teleologically distinct, that they're biologically and mentally suited to their roles. If they are, then the Society is closer to being beautiful. But if such a claim is merely Gold propaganda, then the harmoniousness is merely illusory and thus so is the beauty of the Society. The text of *Red Rising* does not conclusively tell us whether the castes are genuinely teleologically distinct or not, so a definitive answer is hard to reach.

But picking sides on this question is less important than being able to think clearly and carefully about beauty and justice, two of our most important values. For that, the Colors are a fruitful propaedeutic.

12
The Law of *Red Rising*

CHRISTOPHER KETCHAM

In my thought experiment "Forty Hectares and a Mu," the Earth needs Mars to be terraformed, but the costs are so high, economic relations break down between Earth and the emergent Mars. Mars becomes estranged from Earth, and the powerbrokers and wealthy landowners of Mars begin to form their own version of governance.

By the time we get to the first story of *Red Rising*, Mars has evolved its structured caste system from Luna (Earth's moon), as the original seat of its Society. In this hegemonic world the classes are taught, begin to believe, and finally accept the message of the oppressors (the Golds) as their own story. Antonio Gramsci explained in *Selections from the Prison Notebooks* that this is the true nature of hegemony (leadership or dominance by one social group); the oppressed ultimately come to buy into and espouse the message of the oppressor.

Carrying my thought experiment through to *Red Rising*, specifically to the early years after the great divergence between Earth and Mars, how might the laws of Mars have evolved? For this we must turn to the great debate that continues to rage between jurists—whether law is essentially natural or positive.

Prologue to *Red Rising*

In *Leviathan*, Thomas Hobbes distinguished between the *state of nature* and the *state of laws*. In the state of nature *all* are out for themselves. As a result, as he famously said, people live lives that are solitary, poor, nasty, brutish, and short. This is the human state of living feral. The state of laws, according to Hobbes, begins in awe of a common power—like the Golds. However, said Hobbes, "Hereby it is manifest that during the time men live without a common power to keep them all in awe, they are in that condition which is called war; and such a war as is of every man against every man."

John Locke, on the other hand, suggested much the same as Hobbes but allowed for the idea that despite the fact that there's a sovereign to arbitrate laws in the state of laws, some may continue to exist in the state of nature. If, for example, the Golds were to classify Reds as children or slaves, they could justify their hegemonic rule in Lockean terms— Golds live in the state of laws, and Reds exist in a state of nature. The Golds could then require their brand of discipline in order for Reds to ultimately transition into a state of laws—if this might ever be possible. We ask, however, is suppression warranted to get Reds in line and into the state of laws?

In *Red Rising* we see that the Reds have bought into the hegemony of being subaltern slaves to the Golds and all other color-groupings. They hold themselves to their toilsome and often brutal life in the mines. They're generally in awe of the Golds and the hegemonic message that *they*, the Reds, are servant leaders. They're doing the hard work to support humanity's efforts to finish the terraforming of Mars. They've become "enabled martyrs," which leads us right into the discussion of natural law.

Imagine the 1600s of Hobbes's life. The Christian church holds sway over the population. There are two sets of laws to be concerned with—the law of the Church and the civil law. While there's civil law, there is a higher religious law that in many ways outranks the civil law. Many of the precepts of civil law have been adapted from biblical teachings, such as the Ten Commandments. Therefore, in addition to having the usual political discussions between lay people concerning new acts or laws, there's often consultation with the clergy, or a call back to one's own knowledge of the scriptures, to determine whether the civil law will conflict with the teachings of the Church.

Natural law theory holds to the idea that there's a law that is *higher* than the civil law. As such the higher law applies to all, regardless of whether the civil law applies equally to all. If you favor the natural law, then you believe that there is some form of superior law that serves to critique and justify *any* law. Morality and law are intimately linked. Whether a theological critique as proposed by St. Thomas Aquinas, or something based upon community standards, like that of Ronald Dworkin or Hugo Grotius, this higher law approach means you support a type of natural law theory.

Martyrs like the Reds, in some respects, live charmed lives—hear me out. While they may live within the community, even in segregated communities; like others, they've taken upon themselves the burdens of society. The awe for the Christian martyr isn't that of the living sovereign, but God. The Reds are martyrs not to God, the Golds, or Emperor Hirohito—as were the Japanese soldiers of World War II—but to humanity itself. Humanity is the manifestation of the good, whether or not there's a god in the world of *Red Rising*.

The Golds use the mythology of Ares, the god of war, to lump Reds into a single subaltern category. Hegemony favors the categorizing of *all* members of the subaltern category as being associated directly with the *few* who have challenged authority, as did Hitler with his demonization of the Jews, Communists, and other "undesirables." By demonizing the entire group, all Reds can be classified as being dangerous. For a more recent example, during "the troubles" of the latter half of the twentieth century, not all Catholic nationalists in Northern Ireland were members of the violent wings of the Irish Republican Army (IRA), yet the press and politicians in London and elsewhere often categorized Northern Ireland Catholic nationalists as violent revolutionaries. Similarly, there's a group of Reds that call themselves the Sons of Ares, but not all Reds are aptly associated with the moniker.

The Reds' war at the beginning of *Red Rising* is for the "good" of humanity. Their war is against Mars the harsh mistress, not the Golds. However, like all slaves they try to hide their burning hatred for their oppressors from the Golds by focusing it on something else. Often this something else is other Reds as they all compete for the Laurel and the extra rations and meager luxuries that accompany it. Of course, the Laurel is given by the Golds, and it is not really given to the meritorious. The entire competition for the Laurel is simply another clever way for the Golds to continue to keep the Reds toiling away.

In *Red Rising* we have a dual system where the supervening higher law is that of saving humanity, over the oppression of the Golds. In that respect, the supervening law of humanity becomes the Reds' torch to the fire they will use to burn out the oppression of the Golds.

Martian Positive Law?

Natural law has faded from fashion as of late, superseded by a move towards *positive law*, led by the noted jurist H.L.A. Hart. Those in the positive law camp have a problem with the idea of a superior higher law. Hart argued that morality and the law are indeed separate, that the law is posited, and that positive law considers "aims, purposes and policies" associated with the rule of law, legislation and other positive activities. The law is what it is, and interpretations of the law are derived from the law, except when there are circumstances that don't quite fit the law. Hart used the term 'penumbra' to describe such circumstances.

Positive law suggests that morality and the law are separate. But if morality and the law are separate, then Golds can assert the primacy of their statutory and authoritarian laws with impunity. Even if their laws are morally bankrupt and separate from any higher moral or ethical constitution, their laws are what they are, and there's no higher ground on which to disagree.

Adolf Hitler often serves as the poster child for why law and morality are inseparable. However, rather than subvert the idea of the separation of law and morality, Hitler may serve to show how law and morality can be separated. The truth is that the long-developed criminal code in Germany that forbad homicide remained in effect throughout the Third Reich. Run of the mill murderers were prosecuted during the Third Reich as they were before. As noted by Tony Honore, Hitler's atrocities were conducted outside the law. Jews and other "undesirables" were categorized as being outside the law (and inhuman), which allowed Hitler and his henchmen to act with impunity against the now "non-citizen" Jews. Inhumanity doesn't apply if the object of the inhumane treatment isn't classified as being human.

With this we see a difference between the Nazis and the law of *Red Rising*. The oppression of *Red Rising* isn't being carried out by clandestine goon squads through a wink and a nod like the Nazis, nor are Reds summarily considered inhuman. The Golds exhort their subalterns to produce for the good of all humanity. Reds are part of and within the law. They're seen as a necessary component of society, and the harsh laws that oppress them were perhaps originally designed to ensure their eventual freedom.

Law Isn't Moral!

Perhaps the complaint from the positive law theorists begins in the theological taint of the higher law of the past. From Jeremy Bentham and John Austin we get the idea that a law doesn't have to be a good law, or even a moral law, to be a law. Looking back, how could we morally justify the concept of "separate but equal" that became the law of the land as a result of the US Supreme Court decision of *Plessy v. Ferguson* in 1896? Yet, it took until 1954 for the US Supreme Court to reverse *Plessy* with *Brown v. Board of Education*, and that was only to make segregation in the public schools illegal.

From a moral standpoint, Bentham and Austin also could make the case that the Golden Rule is morally desirable, but isn't represented in any law. The laws of *Red Rising* permit the segregation of Colors and justify their treatment as virtual slaves. We might want the Golden Rule to ascend as a law, but alas, while an aspiration, by no means is it the rule of law in *Red Rising*.

By banning demokracy, and enforcing their own brand of caste-based subalternism, the Golds operate a legal system that may not have a basis in a morality we've ever conceived of, but it's still a rule of law. The Golds fear demokracy simply because it embraces the will of the *people*, not merely the will of the Golds. So, the Golds show us that the rule of law doesn't need a moral construct as its underpinning.

Just Another Slaveholding State

Yet what the law of *Red Rising* has produced isn't all that different from the early American democracy. Before the American Revolution, only freeholders who owned land could vote; only representatives of the same could make law. After the Declaration of Independence many states changed their voting rules to give the right to vote to all free men. Women could not vote, and African Americans were classified as slaves, unless they had been freed. However, southern states got the constitutional convention to agree that a slave would count as three-fifths of a human for census purposes. Their logic was that there were fewer whites in the south, which meant they would have fewer representatives in Congress, unless they could count slaves. They didn't want to consider slaves full citizens though, since to do so would invigorate the argument that slaves were indeed persons. Morality teaches that it is wrong to enslave a person. So, the lawmakers used an immoral law to their advantage. *Red Rising*'s system of jurisprudence has many of the same discriminatory features of the early American democracy.

Both early America and *Red Rising* Mars have a caste system based upon an accident of birth that creates a hierarchy of ruling elites, functionaries and slaves. Both used laws to ensure the slaves had no means of rising above their station in life. The main difference between the two is that in *Red Rising*, the Golds use their own brand of propaganda to inculcate Reds with the belief that their slavery is an honorable act of leading humanity towards victory over Mars. For this propaganda to be successful, the Reds' suffering of intolerable conditions as slaves must be seen as a command given to the soldiers in the frontline trenches of a war against the environment of Mars itself. The conditions and command system are just part of the price that humanity must pay to win the war.

On Mars, resistance implies the death of humanity. You're not just revolting against an unjust law, you're committing an act of mutiny against your species. If you're a Red, you're in a state of war, and the only way out of it is to follow the laws set in place by the Golds.

The Real War of *Red Rising*

The Reds are slaves, given nothing but subsistence—or less—for backbreaking work. But like the American slaves, they love to sing and dance—which is tolerable as long as they work and do not use dance or song to complain. Octavia au Lune sings of their struggles, but also of their hegemonic acceptance of their fate to save humanity—to be the ones who produce the helium-3 needed to make Mars a paradise for all. Their work is towards their salvation, she sings, but along the way they must all understand that Red virtue begins in "obedience, respect, sacrifice, and hierarchy." All of these are necessary to win the war against Mars and to reach its promised land—a successfully terraformed surface. Podginus, the Copper administrator, echoes these with his own exhortation, "But order, discipline, and the law. These are the things which empower our race."

The real dilemma of *Red Rising* is that the people on Mars are at war with the planet itself. Mars resists occupation with its lack of a magnetic field to ward off cosmic radiation, bitter cold, giant dust storms, thin atmosphere, and limited liquid water. If the people of Mars are truly at war with Mars, then they're *not* in a *state of law*. They're in a *state of war*, and wars have their own rules. People are commanded during war. Society's laws are changed, morphed, or ignored when the necessities of war conflict. In war, people are commanded to put themselves in harm's way. Some die, others suffer, and all is "fair." Warriors follow commands, whether or not they like or agree with their orders. So, if the Reds are at war with Mars, then the Gold caste system imposed seems like it could be legitimate.

However, there are two worlds on Mars. The Reds exist in a state of war against Mars, and the Golds exist in a near utopia. The Golds make the rules in a state of law, yet for the Reds, the rules take the form of commands in a state of war. The Reds believe they're the warriors, and the Golds feel they're the entitled rulers.

Despite the propaganda, a Red (slave) poses as a Gold to show that all Colors deserve to be treated equally under the law. He used his golden skin color, like many African Americans did, to escape the bondage of slavery imposed by Golds. Herein lies the most important lesson: all must be given a voice, the right to speak.

The legal philosopher H.L.A. Hart, though he rejected the theory of natural law, understood that freedom of speech—freedom to criticize—was necessary to prevent laws from becoming terribly bad. In *Red Rising*, Reds who speak are hanged. Since Reds can't speak freely, whether you're a natural law or a positive law proponent, you can see that the laws are ungrounded. The Golds' legal system excludes many voices, especially Reds, and until all voices are heard, the Golds can't claim to have a morally grounded legal system. The Reds don't have any vote, which means the law can't be morally criticized.

Sitting Where I Want To

Homer Plessy could pass for white, so he boarded a train in Louisiana in the 1890s and sat in the white section. He claimed that being seven-eighths white allowed him the right to sit in the white section, and after being thrown out, he sued claiming discrimination. The Supreme Court in *Plessy v. Ferguson* (1894) said this was wrongheaded thinking because Plessy had no right to claim the *property* of whiteness. The court reasoned that Plessy couldn't claim discrimination or damage to his reputation as a white man, because he was not white. Whiteness and Goldness are property. Property can be passed down. Owners can exclude others from their property, and valuable property—like whiteness and Goldness—give status to property owners. Reds have no such claim to the property of Goldness, because only Golds can pass on the property to other Golds. Darrow is the Mars equivalent of Homer Plessy. If he were able to bring his case before the Supreme Court of Mars, he would receive the same judgment—Darrow has no right to claim the property of Goldness. He'd then be sent back to the mines "where he belongs," or simply executed.

The debate rages on regarding whether there's a moral law that supersedes the civil law, or if there's only the civil law. The positive law theory works only if people have a voice, which the Reds lack. Once people are segregated or segmented into humans and less-than-humans the law devolves into something that is neither natural nor positive. If there's no opportunity for the oppressed to challenge the law, does the law apply to them? This is the squirm in the debate. What happens when the law becomes rotten and those who are at the bottom of the garbage heap can't negotiate their way out?

Are revolution and war the only legitimate cures for the problem? The debate will rage on, both on Earth and Mars, but perhaps future outposts of humanity will retain a strong tether to the legal democratic systems that evolved on Earth starting in the eighteenth century.

IV

The Rising and Beyond

13
Mustang's Future Generations

CourtLAND Lewis

Pierce Brown's *Red Rising* trilogy is a tale of humanity's possible future. As humanity begins to colonize other planets, they quickly run into the need for more and more life-sustaining resources, especially when terraforming the surface of Mars.

The only way to sustain life on Mars (and other terraformed planets) is helium-3, and lowReds are asked to slave as miners for the health and salvation of future generations. Is it just to ask a people to live as slaves in order for future generations to thrive? Would it be more just to let everyone live and consume all they want, and let future generations be damned?

If we contrast the beginning with the end of the trilogy, where Mustang, Darrow, and the others in charge must figure out who'll bear the burdens of the Society, in order to ensure the existence of future generations, then we're faced with some difficult questions. Who's going to work in the mines, who's going to cook, clean, and do the jobs that no one else wants? What sort of policies should they enact to ensure the existence of future generations, and what sort of obligations do they have towards them? Heck, do they have any obligations towards future generations? Is there a political or moral principle, or set of principles, we can follow to ensure we make the right decisions?

The truth is, many of the answers to these and similar questions will depend on who you ask, and what sort of "future generation" they have in mind. When I say "future generations," do you think of your kids, grandkids, and other people closely related to your current existence, or do you think of the millions of unknown people who will (hopefully) exist in a thousand years?

Eo is concerned with the latter group. She sacrifices her own life, and the life of her child, so that the entire Society can be liberated from the Golds. I assume not many would sacrifice so much for the good of millions of unknown future people, though some might sacrifice themselves for a loved one's future happiness.

Can any of these sacrifices be rationally justified? Philosophy provides some interesting answers about what sort of obligations we have towards future generations. As we'll see, many of them are strange and complex, but they're well-worth the effort. So, let's see if we can help Mustang figure out a way to create a Society that cares for its current citizens while also caring for future generations.

Future Fortunate Sons

Making decisions about future generations might not seem that difficult, but after a few illustrations, you'll see it's as thorny as a nest of pitvipers. Moral theories are grounded in some claim of value. Once a moral value is assumed, ethicists create a consistent decision-making procedure for what is morally right and wrong.

For instance, if good character is your moral value, then your moral theory will explain what counts as "good character," and explain how a person can live in such a way as to develop such character. If rationality is your moral value, then you might formulate how rationality creates duties between all rational agents; or you might suggest that only rational agents can enter into moral contracts, and these contracts ground a set of particular rights and corresponding obligations. Finally (though there are many more we could consider), if pleasure and pain are your moral values, then your moral theory will describe how certain actions are moral or immoral because of the amounts of pleasure and pain they produce.

These possibilities are brief sketches of four major ethical theories (virtue, duty ethics, Contractarian rights, and utilitarianism), and though they all do a good job (some better than others) at providing ethical people with sound moral advice about how to act and live their lives today, they fail to explain how to treat future generations.

The problem of future generations is that they don't exist, and their not existing wreaks havoc on many of the basic assumptions of our moral theories. For instance, if Darrow truly believes that all people have the same moral worth, regardless of their Color, then this means that all rational individuals should treat each other with mutual respect. Such a moral position is laudable, but it doesn't help us with future generations. Future generations don't exist, and nonexistent things lack rationality, so they lack the moral feature that would make them deserving of respect.

The same holds true if we try to base moral worth on contractual agreements between rational people. Non-existent people can't enter into contracts. Darrow can make moral agreements about how to structure society that applies to future generations, like building nature preserves on Mars, but such agreements are not made with future generations— they're made with current generations. In fact, our assumption that future generations would want nature preserves is merely based on our current belief that preserves have some value in Society. Future generations might not care for preserves at all, and because future generations don't exist, they can't say what they would like or dislike. So, neither pure rationality nor moral contracts apply to future generations.

Another option is to rely on good character. Mustang serves as a good example of someone with a virtuous character. She seems to conduct her life with honesty, empathy, courage, and integrity. For Mustang it's easy to exhibit such qualities to the people she meets on a daily basis, but how can she do so with future generations? Future generations don't exist, so it's impossible to exhibit good character to them.

Mustang might imagine future generations, and how she wants to create a good Society for them to exist in, but as Derek Parfit suggests in *Reason and Persons*, once we make a decision that affects a future generation, we destroy that future generation by creating a new one. If Darrow had decided to sacrifice himself at the beginning of *Red Rising*, to ensure his clan would get the Laurel, then he would've destroyed the future generations we read about in *Golden Son* and *Morning Star*.

Life's full of such decisions. The conceptual difficulty is that each new future generation we create will have its own issues that we must then address. But as soon as we try to address them, we create a new future generation with its own problems, which we must then address. So trying to imagine future generations and make allowances for their specific needs is a futile activity. Of course, we might get lucky with some broad general allowances, like ensuring clean air, but all decisions come with a set of costs. Choosing to dedicate resources to providing the future with clean air means that we can't dedicate resources to some other problem. So, either way, we leave them with problems. So much for the virtue approach.

Finally, if pleasure and pain are the basis of your morality, then you can't say that what you're doing today will—or won't—bring about your desired pleasure for future generations. Such a utilitarian approach offers solutions to the question of near-future generations, but fails when considering distant-future generations. For example, the Jackal attempts to nuke Luna, which readers are supposed to consider bad. For near-future generations of Luna his actions are obviously bad. Millions of people will suffer and die, radiation will destroy the environment, and many birth anomalies and defects will result. However, since we're dealing with the future, which no one knows, we don't know if the Jackal's success might have brought about a better future in the extreme long-term. Since we're using our imagination, we can imagine a future where the Jackal's failure leads to an even more dysfunctional Society than the one we read about in the trilogy. We can also imagine a future where the Jackal's success leads to great prosperity and freedom. Because we don't know the future, until Brown decides to write another series of books, we simply can't say that our current actions will produce our long-term desired results.

Parfit's Total Institute Challenge

Even with its shortcoming, many felt that a utilitarian approach to future generations was best. That is, until Derek Parfit did some philosophical "reaping" in the 1980s with his book *Reasons and Persons*. In this ground-breaking book he presents readers with a set of thought experiments that challenge the core of moral philosophy, especially in regards to future generations. Let's see how you might solve Parfit's thought experiments.

Say, you're Darrow or Mustang, and you're tasked with adopting social policies that will maximize the pleasure of future generations. The key question is: Do you maximize the total amount (quantity) of pleasure or the average amount (quality) of pleasure? Deciding between the two might not seem that important at first glance, but choosing one or the other will create drastically different outcomes. Look at the chart on the next page, and imagine the numbers are units of pleasure.

With this handy chart, we see that if you focus on total pleasure, then you will choose policies that bring about world C, but if you're interested in average pleasure, then the policies that bring about world A come the closest to creating a world where everyone is close to the average amount of pleasure. See how different the outcomes are depending on whether you focus on quantity over quality (and vice versa).

Let's say you're more like the Jackal and you want as much total pleasure as possible. So, if you have to choose between policies that bring about two future worlds, you'll

World:	A	B	C
Darrow	6	8	2
Mustang	5	7	1
Jackal	1	0	18
Total:	12	15	21
Average:	4.3	5	7

choose the one with the greater quantity of whatever makes life worth living. If world A has 100 units of pleasure, and world B has 200, then you will choose world B, and if world C has 201, then you will choose world C. The basis of your decision—maximize total pleasure—and reason alone dictate that you choose the world with more pleasure, no matter what.

As Parfit points out, such a logic has devastating consequences, for we can always imagine adding more people to the equation, thereby increasing total pleasure. Sure, with more people added, everyone's individual pleasure goes down a little, but by adding more people you increase the overall total amount of pleasure. So, if world B is better than world A, because it has a greater quantity of pleasure resulting from more people added, and world C has more people than world B, then world C is better than world B.

The logic of total pleasure requires us to pick policies that will create a world where we have the maximum amount of people, and even though everyone has barely any pleasure, the total amount of pleasure will exceed all other possible worlds. If you think about it, this sounds a lot like the world of *Red Rising*, where even the life of Reds (and other low Colors) is worth living, though only barely. However, to really achieve the world Parfit imagines, all you would need is a few more billion people, and all Colors would need to live lives similar to that of the Reds. Like most readers, Parfit finds such a world repugnant, which is why he says that focusing on policies that bring about total pleasure leads to the "Repugnant Conclusion" of ever-increasing population and decreased individual pleasure.

The principle of utility and reason tell us to pick the world with the maximum amount of people, whose lives are barely worth living, but intuition tells us to pick a world somewhere in between that and a world with no people. You could pick somewhere in between, but you would need to back your selection with good reasons. The world of maximum population is repugnant, but it's backed by sound reasoning. Your desire to avoid the repugnant world is (at least so far) merely based on intuitions and emotional feelings. You need a set of rationally justified moral reasons that say your desired future in between world is the right world to create, and we've yet to discover them. You might want to ask, "Who cares?", but if you do, then you have no grounds on which to criticize the Golds for their population policies, since they too simply picked a world in between.

Who Wants to Be Average?

Let's back up. If total utility doesn't work, then maybe we should choose average utility. According to Parfit, however, choosing average utility leads to the "mere addition paradox," which says that it's always worse to add a group of people whose quality of life is slightly below average, no matter how high the average of the other population. This paradox would make Roque's head hurt, so I'm going to keep it as simple as possible. Using a diagram from John Nolt, if height represents quality of pleasure, and width quantity, we can imagine the following worlds:

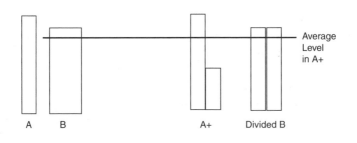

In the diagram, if you were choosing policies that brought about a higher average pleasure, A is better than B because it has a higher average of pleasure, even though B has more total pleasure. If such reasoning is applied consistently throughout, you'd arrive at the following conclusions. A has the highest quality of pleasure. B and Divided B are the same. A+ is worse than both Divided B and B, because the latter two have a higher average utility. B is worse than A, and finally, A+ is worse than A.

Let's try to make sense of these conclusions. Parfit wants to show that merely adding something to a calculation of pleasure doesn't negatively affect the quality of pleasure. Imagine that Mustang institutes policies that make humanity's pleasure equal to that of A. Unbeknownst to Mustang, a civilization of humanoids in the Andromeda galaxy creates their own Society, and their quality of pleasure is much lower than A. In fact, their pleasure equals the amount of the second bar on A+. So, if A+ represents Mustangs Society (the bar on the left) and Andromeda's Society (the bar on the right), then by adding Andromeda's pleasure we lower the average utility of Mustang's Society. Yet, the pleasure of Mustang's Society stays the same! The paradox, then, is that their pleasure is the same, yet according to the logic of average pleasure, they are worse off. I told you it was complicated!

As a result, Parfit maintains that we should reject relying on average pleasure too, since it leads to a logical contradiction—it can't be true that Mustang's Society is both the same and worse-off at the same time.

As you can imagine many have argued against Parfit and his conclusions, but instead of trotting out a bunch of counterarguments, I want to focus on a possible solution.

Pure Procedural Rising

John Rawls created his own revolution in moral philosophy by establishing a "pure procedural" approach to justice. Put simply, a pure procedural approach allows people the opportunity to make rational moral decisions without being tainted by the random biases of race, gender, ethnicity, or Color. When you're free from the biases of your own particular factors of life, you're in what Rawls calls "the original position." As Rawls explains in *A Theory of Justice*, *Political Liberalism*, and *Justice as Fairness*, the original position can be achieved by "stepping behind" the veil of ignorance. The veil is a conceptual tool for helping people make decisions about how best to morally structure society.

More specifically, what happens behind the veil is that agents become self-interested "maximin-ers" (as in, maximize the minimum). A maximin-er will choose outcomes that *maximize* the social conditions of the least advantaged (or worse-off) individuals in society—those who have the *minimum*. For instance, imagine if the Sovereign stepped behind the veil and considered how to structure society. She might first consider the Color-caste system. Should we have a system where Golds rule in luxury and Reds are slave laborers? As a Gold, she might be tempted to say that we should keep the Society how it's currently structured. However, behind the veil of ignorance, she doesn't know she's a Gold. For all she knows, she might be a Red or a Pink! In fact, behind the veil she doesn't even know she's female.

So, when considering what rules should structure society, a rational self-interested person would only pick rules that benefit everyone fairly, and wouldn't pick any rule that would overly disadvantage anyone. This is why Rawls calls his theory of justice "justice as fairness." Since, no rational self-interested person would choose to be enslaved, the Sovereign wouldn't choose the Society's caste system.

Rawls's procedure wasn't designed to see into the future, but it was designed to create social structures that would protect the least advantaged and evolve over time, as new moral challenges arise. For him, the following two moral principles will result from the original position:

1. Each person has an equal right to the most extensive scheme of equal basic liberties compatible with a similar scheme of liberties for all.

2. Social and economic inequalities are permissible provided that they are: a. to the greatest expected benefit of the least advantaged; and b. attached to positions and offices open to all under conditions of fair equality of opportunity.

Armed with these two principles of justice, all moral agents in a society, no matter their Color, should be free to pursue their individual conceptions of the good. Hence, justice and politics become a matter of maintaining a fair *procedure* for deciding the distribution of societal benefits and burdens. By focusing on creating a current fair procedure that evolves over time, for Rawls, we create a process by which we justly care for future generations by ensuring society is always structured fairly.

To create such a procedure we must address what the philosopher Tim Mulgan calls the "just savings problem." Like all societies, Mustang must balance investment in the future against current consumption. If Mustang's Society consumes everything, then subsequent generations will be left with nothing and will starve. If the Society consumes exactly as much as they produce, then subsequent generations will face the same situation as the first generation. They will all survive, but they will never experience progress. Finally, if the Society produces and saves more than they consume, then current generations will suffer, but subsequent generations will be better off.

Which option is the most just? For Rawls, option one, where the Society consumes everything and leaves nothing for future generations, is immoral. You'd have to be completely apathetic to the plight of others, be willing to allow and endure great suffering of others, and hold a complete disregard for the life of future generations to accept option one. This appears to be what the Gold-framers of the Society had in mind, except they tried to make it where only future Golds would prosper. Of course, the reasons listed against option one are based on mere intuitions, and as we've discussed above, we'd prefer something more substantial—in other words, something supported by logical reasoning.

One solution is to focus on the well-grounded moral principle that it's immoral to cause unnecessary suffering. Option one implies that you're willing to let *all* future generations suffer, which includes near generations that will actually exist during your lifetime. So, option one implies a willingness to watch actual people suffer unnecessarily. Due to the nature of the decision, which affects everyone born after the decision is made, option one violates a well-justified moral position that it's immoral to purposely cause or allow the unnecessary suffering of others. So, we can make a fairly strong case, which provides a logic-based reason for rejecting option one.

Option two is fairly harmless—all generations do just enough to get by, so all future generations have the same advantages and disadvantages. If Mustang were to choose this, then she'd surely be guilty of doing nothing immoral. In fact, for the immediate future of the Society, this might be her only option. With the amount of destruction and social upheaval, people won't have much time for accumulating resources. They'll be doing their best to stay alive. However, after a period they will begin to prosper again, and Mustang will need to determine if there's a better option.

Option three, to produce more than what is consumed, and leave future generations better-off, appears to be the best option for all future generations. The problem with this option is that it asks current generations to sacrifice for future generations. Is such sacrifice just? Those who are well-off in the Society won't be affected much, but the worse-off in the Society could suffer greatly, because instead of using all resources to improve the lives of the worse-off on Mars and on the Outer Rim planets, resources are put aside for the benefit of future generations. So, option three sounds a lot like telling Reds that they must suffer now for the sake of humanity in the future. This is a tricky problem, but it's not insurmountable.

To reply to this criticism the reader must keep in mind that Rawls is concerned with a theory of justice, not benefi-cence, and that the original position is only theoretical. It's true that there are always individuals and groups that are worse-off than others. Each society has its Reds. However, Rawls's theory of justice suggests that people in the original position are moral equals, such that we all must consider ourselves as one of the worse-off.

Furthermore, to fully reply to the complaint that current generations will be worse-off than future generations, we have to note the vagueness of term 'worse-off'. When we speak of future generations being "worse-off," we're making assumptions about their level of autonomy, the sort of society that will exist, and the technology that will exist. Yet, as we have seen, future generations don't exist. So we can't truly say they're worse-off for not getting to choose their fate, for not having certain advantages, and for not having certain technologies.

When we speak of current generations being worse-off with respect to autonomy, material goods, and technology we're making assumptions about the future which we can't know. Sacrifices made by humans in the early 1900s led to great advances in computing and technology, but the people had no idea they were "worse-off," nor in what way they were worse-off. In other words, the American farmers of the early 1900s didn't lament their lack of GPS technology. They were more worried about how to improve productivity, pre-serve food, and maintain the land. Yet, through their activ-ities they directly and indirectly "suffered" (though they might not have considered it suffering) so that society could be better-off, even though it turned out vastly different than expected.

One of the key moral components here is intentions. To achieve option three, Mustang must pick just policies with the intent that current generations will benefit slightly (or only suffer slightly), and future generations will benefit greatly. For Rawls, as long as her decisions are designed to benefit all, then they are just. Even if historical occurrences prevent current generations from prospering, and produce future generations that are worse-off, justice only requires that Mustang's current decision be just when she makes it. The justness of her decision can't be judged on yet unknown facts and knowledge.

To look at it another way, Rawls's theory of justice is concerned with making the basic structure of society "fair"—in other words, just. From Rawls's original position, future generations are merely future current generations. So if given the same set of facts about how best to govern the Society, every generation would make the same decision behind the veil of ignorance. In other words, all generations are *theoretically* advantaged/disadvantaged in the same respect. Since all generations are in the same position, and would prefer that both current and future generations prosper, then option three appears to be the fairest choice in the original position.

Howler Repugnancy

Rawls's procedural justice seems to answer the just savings problem, but Tim Mulgan argues that Rawls's solution leads back to Parfit's Repugnant Conclusion. For Mulgan, it's unclear whether a future generation can disagree with Mustang's decision to use option three, because any other savings rate would have produced different individuals causing those who exist in the future not to exist. In other words, when the population created by Mustang's decisions considers what should be done in the original positon, they will agree. To disagree is to say it's better not to exist—an existential quandary indeed! So, for Mulgan, the original position is unattainable because each generation must consider the just savings decision of the previous generation the just decision. As a result, each generation is forced to maximize pleasure for future generations, which eventually leads to the repugnant conclusion—a gigantic population with lives barely worth living.

There's one fatal flaw in Mulgan's argument. Parfit's repugnant conclusion is a conceptual truth, one that sheds light on the soundness of our moral reasoning. Apart from telling us not to use utilitarianism to make policy decisions about future generations, it doesn't provide specific guidance for how to make actual policy decisions. The repugnant conclusion could never actually occur in real life, since every planet has a certain carrying capacity, at which the planet will no longer support life. It might get close, similar to what happens in the Society of *Red Rising*, but the planet would collapse (or self-correct) long before reaching the world of the repugnant conclusion.

To see how this works in real life, think of deer populations. If left alone, deer will multiply to such an extent that the forest can't sustain their existence. As a result of an ever-increasing population, many deer will starve and die, but the strongest and fastest (and whatever other advantages deer have, like the ability to stay off of highways!) deer will survive. So, there's a natural check on how many deer will live and die. The repugnant conclusion, however, ignores these natural checks, and suggests a conceptual world where deer don't die. Their populations keep growing and growing.

Humans have their own carrying capacity, and even though humans are good at creating technologies to overcome our capacities, there are limits. Science fiction like *Red Rising* is good at imagining and testing these limits. Nevertheless, it seems impossible to actually reach Parfit's envisioned repugnant conclusion—though the future may show otherwise—and if it's impossible, then no generation can favor creating a world seen in the repugnant conclusion.

They might enact policies that get close, but if guided by Rawls's principles of justice, they'll avoid getting too close.

So, if Mustang picks option three and uses Rawls's original position to make decisions, she (and all others) should be guided to support maximum sustainability practices beneficial to all generations. Sure, the current generation might suffer more than some future generations, but Rawls's principles of justice will require that any suffering be distributed fairly across the Society. So, it can't just be put on the backs of a few Colors!

In fact, for Rawls, option three's stable sustainable society appears to be the most desirable and just societal goal. As he describes in *Justice as Fairness*, justice "does not require continual economic growth over generations to maximize . . . the expectations of the least advantaged." Societal justice isn't about accumulating more wealth, which often leads to the practices of *Red Rising*, where several lower classes carry the burden of the wealthy. Instead, societal justice requires creating a fair system of social engagement that "evens out" existing or emerging inequalities within the system, so all can flourish.

Mustang's task is monumental, but if she uses Rawls's original position to solve the just savings problem and to institute fair policies for future generations, she will have set the Society on the road to a bright, prosperous, and just future. She will have also created a set of policies and societal practices that all generations, past, present, and future, will agree are worthy of protecting.

14
Guns Don't Kill Colors—
Colors Kill Colors

Robert Arp

The rifle itself has no moral stature, since it has no will of its own. Naturally, it may be used by evil men for evil purposes, but there are more good men than evil, and while the latter cannot be persuaded to the path of righteousness by propaganda, they can certainly be corrected by good men with rifles.

—Jeff Cooper, *The Art of the Rifle* (1997)

The president of the Colt Patent Fire Arms Co., Fred A. Roff Jr., noted in a May 31st 1959 article from Pasadena's *Independent Star-News*: "Our big concern is to make sure that guns get into the hands of only those who know how to use them. Guns don't kill people. People kill people."

There are plenty of people in this world who would agree with Roff, but there are also those who see guns and other armaments as inherently sinister things that wreak havoc all over the place, almost having minds of their own. In a *Slate* article from August of 2012, former New York governor and admitted philanderer, Eliot Spitzer, captures this sentiment: "Yes, people pull the trigger—but guns are the instrument of death. Gun control is necessary, and delay means more death and horror." These people are usually called *gun control advocates*.

In Pierce Brown's *Red Rising* trilogy many weapons are used. Obsidians are crafted as brutal weapons of war, Golds use razors, gravBoots, pulseFists, and ghostCloaks to retain power, and the Sons of Ares use explosives and other means of war to spread their terror. Of course, the most prominent weapon is Darrow himself, whom the Sons create to destroy Gold Society. How, then, should we respond to the existence of so many weapons? Should we get rid of them all, including Darrow? Would it help the Reds, Pinks, Browns, and other Colors that suffer under the might of the Golds, or would it make their oppression worse?

In order to protect yourself from others (including the government) in a social setting, it's necessary to have the option of utilizing lethal force, and a gun is one such type of force. You probably guessed it, but I'm the opposite of a gun control advocate; I'm a *gun rights advocate*.

Justifiably Preserving Yourself and Another

"Self-preservation is a typical property of living organisms, observed in the simplest prokaryotic cell as well as in the more complex multicellular organisms." So claim the researchers in an article about the self-preservation of an anti-cancer enzyme from *The Biochemical Journal* in November of 2003.

However, it's not merely the case *that* self-preservation is a basic feature of any organism, it's also the case that living things *should* preserve their lives. Thomas Hobbes (1588–1679) penned his great book *Leviathan* in 1651, and this work is usually referenced as the basis for social contract theory. During a discussion of rights and the obligation associated with self-preservation, Hobbes notes:

THE RIGHT OF NATURE, which Writers commonly call *Jus Naturale*, is the Liberty each man hath, to use his own power, as he will himself, for the preservation of his own Nature; that is to say, of his own Life; and consequently, of doing any thing, which in his own Judgment, and Reason, he shall conceive to be the aptest means thereunto . . .

> A LAW OF NATURE, (*Lex Naturalis*) is a Precept, or general Rule,
> found out by Reason, by which a man is forbidden to do, that,
> which is destructive of his life, or taketh away the means of pre-
> serving the same; and to omit, that, by which he thinketh it may be
> best preserved.

So, from the instinct of self-preservation, it's easy to formulate a general rule regarding self-defense in order to assure
this self-preservation—even if it means that one organism
has to kill another in defense.

Living things want to live, and they should live without
having their lives cut short by some other aggressive force,
especially if that force is taking a life for reasons that are
self-serving or unjust in some way. Pinks shouldn't have to
live their lives in constant fear of being raped and abused.
They want to be free from such threats, and we would support them having the means by which to protect themselves
from aggressors.

Having a set of laws to protect them would be great, but
not everyone follows the law. The Institute has rules, but
most of them are ignored. Just ask those who were raped,
killed, and eaten—oh wait, you can't! If they'd had some way
to protect themselves, then maybe they could've avoided
their awful fate.

Further, from the instinct of self-preservation, it's easy
to formulate another general rule regarding coming to the
defense of another, especially an innocent living thing,
when its life is being threatened in an unjust manner. We
cheer for the dolphin that kills the shark while protecting
her baby, or the second cobra who joins the fight against the
mongoose, or the little old man who puts a bullet in the guy
who's attempting to murder his wife in their bed. So too, we
think that the guy who hits and shakes a crying baby to
death deserves the death penalty, or that the mom who
leaves her infant in a 120-degree car to boil to death while
she shops at Walmart needs to have something similar happen to her, or that the sh@tkicker who drags a cat behind
his pickup truck and joyrides around town for the fun of it

should be castrated with a serrated knife and *without* any anesthesia.

Think you're too good, or above such feelings? How did you feel when Aja, the Sovereign, and the Jackal were finally killed? Did you rejoice in their deaths, or maybe you felt their end came too quick? Unless you were sad that they were finally exterminated, then you probably think, like most readers, that they "deserved it."

The (Im)morality of Pacifism

Killing in self-defense when your life truly is threatened seems justified from almost any point of view—except, perhaps, from some extreme form of *absolute* pacifism. The great Catholic philosopher and theologian, St. Augustine (354–430 C.E.), was opposed to killing in self-defense because he thought it was self-centered and sinful, noting, "Private self-defense can only proceed from some degree of inordinate self-love." However, even the most pacifistic of Buddhists—the folks who come to mind as likely candidates for pacifism—would think that you should try and preserve your life when someone else is trying to take it unjustly. Even though the first of the Five Precepts from Theravada Buddhism (around 400 B.C.E.) notes that "I undertake the training rule to abstain from killing," if it's a kill or be killed situation, even the most devout Buddhist will kill.

Darrow confronts such a problem in the Passage. He doesn't want to kill Julian, but when faced with the possibility of kill or be killed, he kills Julian. Of course, he spends the rest of the trilogy dealing with the consequences of his decision, but it's doubtful any reader feels that Darrow should've allowed himself to be killed.

Concerning killing in defense of another, the existentialist philosopher, Albert Camus (1913–1960), said something similar in a letter applying for conscientious objector status in 1943: "There are perhaps many causes worth dying for, but to me, certainly, there are none worth killing for." Now, it's one thing to choose not to defend your own life in a situation, it's quite another to not defend an innocent from an aggressor. Many would say that not killing someone so as to defend another innocent living thing, especially a human being, is itself immoral!

Imagine trying everything possible to prevent the fate of one of the many children who are raped and murdered in the trilogy—restraining the guy, punching him, biting him—but nothing works, and he continues to proceed with the dirty deeds. Furthermore, imagine you have the opportunity to save the children by killing someone like Aja, but your pacifistic views prevent you from wasting her. Who in their right mind would ever be morally comfortable with that decision?

Or consider serial killers like Jeffrey Dahmer, Ted Bundy, or John Wayne Gacy. If your only option is to kill them before they murder their innocent victims and you don't do it, aren't you in a sense responsible for the deaths of these innocents? Finally, who could have allowed Hitler and the Third Reich to carry out the Final Solution of exterminating all Jews? We feel compelled to assist innocents who are being harmed, we recognize that we have a moral obligation to assist them, we praise those who are able to assist, and do, and we blame those who could assist, but don't.

Double Trouble?

There's an old principle that many of us may not have heard of by name, but still understand well enough called the *principle of double effect*. It's the idea that you can be justified in bringing about some harm or evil result—even killing someone or lots of people—provided that the evil result 1. is not directly intended and 2. isn't greater than the good result that *is* intended.

There are two effects, results, or consequences then; one (single) is a great or greater good that's intended, while the second (double) is a lesser evil that isn't intended. It's a controversial principle because oftentimes we *know* that there's going to be an evil effect that results from one of our actions, even though we don't intend it directly. Well-known actions—

some controversial—where the principle of double effect is utilized include:

Action	Intended Good (Single) Effect, Result, Consequence	Unintended Bad (Double) Effect, Result, Consequence
Performing a risky medical operation	Remove tumor, or fix disorder, or cure disease	Infection occurs, or heart stops during operation and kills the patient
Worker blows whistle on corrupt business practice	Stopping corrupt business practice	Business actually closes down, hundreds of workers lose their jobs
Bombing a terrorist group's installation to destroy armaments	Getting rid of armaments that have been/will be used to kill innocent people	In bombing process, people in the installation are killed
Sergeant jumps on top of a grenade in his squad's tent	Using your body to shield the squad from the blast so as to save lives	Sergeant is killed by grenade
Hysterectomy to remove cancerous tumors	Removing cancer, saving woman's life	Fallopian tubes are removed, woman had ectopic pregnancy, embryo is killed
Giving large dosage of pain killer to terminal patient	Relieve someone from pain and suffering	Patient dies of overdose

While talking about self-defense in his famous work titled *Summa Theologica*, the great Christian philosopher, St. Thomas Aquinas (1225–1274), formulated a version of the principle that is still utilized by people, governments, judicial systems, and religions all over the world today: "Nothing hinders one act from having two effects, only one of which is intended, while the other is beside the intention . . . Accordingly, the act of self-defense may have two effects: one, the saving of one's life; the other, the slaying of the aggressor." So, for example, when the Jackal is going to kill everyone on Luna in *Red Rising*, and Darrow defends them by pulling out the Jackal's tongue and having the flagship destroyed, as long as Darrow intended to protect the innocent life on Luna by destroying the flagship, then the double effect of the flagship being destroyed (which is a great evil, since other innocent people lost their lives) is wholly justified and not unethical or immoral.

Stand Your Ground

A person who is not engaged in an unlawful activity and who is attacked in any other place where he or she has a right to be, has no duty to retreat and has the right to stand his or her ground and meet force with force, including deadly force, if he or she reasonably believes it is necessary to do so to prevent death or great bodily harm to himself or herself or another or to prevent the commission of a forcible felony.

The above quotation is the essence of the so-called *stand-your-ground law* from chapter 776 of the 2011 Florida Statutes (*776.013: Home protection; use of deadly force; presumption of fear of death or great bodily harm*) that Florida and several other US States have adopted. It's a type of self-defense law that gives someone the right to use deadly force to defend herself or himself without any requirement to evade or retreat from a dangerous situation. Your typical gun control advocate has a problem with utilizing a gun in self-defense in general, but *definitely* has a problem with stand-your-ground laws. The reason for this is that given the "reasonable belief" part of the law, someone can use this deadly force based upon the *perception of* imminent danger—essentially, if I *think* my life is in danger as a result of your actions, I can kill you and legally get away with it. The Trayvon Martin case from 2012-2013 comes to mind as a controversial case where George Zimmerman claimed, and the jury agreed, that he thought Martin was going to kill him, so he felt that he had no choice but to shoot Martin with the Kel-Tec 9mm pistol he was carrying.

Your typical gun rights advocate will respond that, despite controversial situations like the shooting of Trayvon Martin and others where it's questionable whether someone's life was truly in danger, the self-defense laws of a society are a necessity as an extension of the general moral or ethical rules regarding self-defense and defense of another, which themselves are grounded in the natural law and right of self-preservation. The following figure illustrates these relationships.

Given these dependencies, argues the gun rights advocate, you must have the option of utilizing lethal force in a social setting to preserve your life or another's life, and a firearm is one such type of force. Gary Kleck and Marc Gertz point out something that may seem self-evident to most people, but is nevertheless crucial to mention:

> If self-protection with a gun is commonplace, it means that any form of gun control that disarms large numbers of prospective victims, either altogether, or only in certain times and places where victimization might occur, will carry significant social costs in terms of lost opportunities for self-protection.

So, when someone says, "I've got a right to defend myself" it's usually the case that if you pressed them for the reasons they think they have this right, they'll ultimately say something like, "Well, I've got a right to preserve my own life, and there's nothing wrong with me trying to preserve it against someone who's trying to kill me, even if I have to kill them in the process."

And this line of thinking seems wholly reasonable to most people, even the gun control advocate, if she or he thinks about it. Gun control advocates, just like gun rights advocates, or anyone else: want to preserve their lives from aggressors; think they should be able to preserve their lives from aggressors; and think that the laws of a society should reflect this.

The Equalizer

> And therefore, if any two men desire the same thing, which nevertheless they cannot both enjoy, they become enemies; and in the way to their end (which is principally their own conservation, and sometimes their delectation only) endeavour to destroy or subdue one another.

—THOMAS HOBBES, *Leviathan* (1651), Chapter XIII

The sad fact of the matter is that certain people will be aggressive enough to kill other people for any of a variety of reasons; this is a point so obvious that it need not even be mentioned. The good news, however, is that there are times when bad people are prevented from carrying out their murderous intentions by being killed through self-defense or defense of another.

There are people who are always naturally at a disadvantage because of their physical stature or circumstances. For instance, Pinks are genetically bred to provide pleasure, not to defend themselves against others. But when you strap an explosive to a Pink, in order to blow up a café, or put a scorcher in their hands, Pinks gain the ability to fight back.

Certain weapons are necessary, then, to counter this disadvantage. Google "Woman defends herself with gun," and you'll be presented with dozens of news articles where single women, old women, and mothers were able to prevent muggers from mugging them, rapists from raping them, and killers from killing them or their children by brandishing a gun or shooting the aggressors dead. Many gun control advocates will say that there are several ways the disadvantaged can protect themselves: rape whistles, self-defense classes, mace, and other things besides a firearm. But these things and methods are still no match for an aggressor who's intent upon doing evil or inflicting harm.

The bottom line is that we all have an inalienable right to protect ourselves and others from aggressors trying to kill or rape us, whether it's through using our fists, a rock, a heavy stick, a knife, a sword, or a gun. We'd even be perfectly justified in using a bomb or something bigger to protect ourselves or others from evil pricks—whatever does the trick. At present, a handgun, like a semi-automatic pistol, is a most effective form of self-defense. It's easy to use, inexpensive, concealable, and even little old ladies can be trained to handle it safely.

Just think how different *Red Rising* would be if every Red and Pink had weapons to defend themselves. People of all Colors would be able to protect themselves, no matter their physical disadvantages. Granted, giving lower Colors a bunch of weapons doesn't mean there would be no more unwanted violence, but it would help even the odds. In fact, *Red Rising* shows us that when given weapons, people are not only able to protect themselves from other individuals, but they're also able to protect themselves from oppressive police states.

Preventing Police States

When dictators come to power, the first thing they do is take away the people's weapons.

—RONALD REAGAN, *Guns & Ammo* (1975)

History has shown time and time again that a disarmed population is simply more likely to be oppressed, exploited, unjustly harmed, or murdered by its government than is an armed citizenry.

When only the police have guns in a society, it's called a *police state*, and we all know what atrocities have occurred in police states like the totalitarian regimes of the Soviet Union, Nazi Germany, the People's Republic of China during the middle of the last century, Cuba and North Korea today, and, in Pierce Brown's future, the Society. What's the first thing a dictator or oligarchic regime does when trying to seize power? Take all the guns.

For example, by 1550 the Japanese had purchased and made improvements on thousands of Portuguese matchlock muskets, which were used by lords and peasants in various military conquests. In August of 1588 the Japanese dictator with the biggest army, Toyotomi Hideyoshi, put forward and enforced an edict called the Sword Hunt (*taiko no katanagari*):

> The people of the various provinces are strictly forbidden to have in their possession any swords, short swords, bows, spears, firearms, or other types of arms. The possession of unnecessary implements makes difficult the collection of taxes and dues and tends to foment uprisings.

Heads of provinces, official agents, and deputies were ordered to collect all of the weapons and hand them over to the

Government. Predictably, Hideyoshi and his successors preceded to commit atrocities against the nobility and especially the peasantry. The samurai were servants of the Japanese leadership, and they were not only allowed to carry swords, but they were given free rein to slaughter peasants for minor offenses, as well as take land, livestock, goods, valuables, and women from the peasantry whenever they wanted to.

But surely this is just a result of medieval times, right? Unfortunately, no. In 1935 Joseph Stalin also imposed a law that made the possession of a weapon (saber, firearm, or knife) punishable by death for anyone twelve years of age and older. Between 1924 and 1953—when Stalin ruled— some forty to sixty million people were displaced and left to starve to death, worked to death, deceived into signing their own death warrants, tortured to death, or outright murdered by Stalin's cronies. Undoubtedly, this thirty-year mass murder was made simpler by the fact that the people had been disarmed.

In the Society, Golds are the only ones with free rein to carry and use weapons, especially the Razor. Obsidians are allowed certain tools, like gravBoots and pulseFists, but they are taught to revere razors as a tool of the gods. Other Colors are strictly forbidden to have, use, or even touch weapons. In a world that fears uprising to the extent that singing the wrong song is deserving of execution, weapons are strictly forbidden. If all Colors had a right to bear arms, things would be drastically different—Golds would have something to fear.

The Society's Second Amendment

Both oligarch and tyrant mistrust the people, and therefore deprive them of arms.

—ARISTOTLE, *The Politics*

Aware of the atrocities perpetrated by the Axis Powers, FDR and the US Congress passed laws that allowed the President to requisition certain property from Americans for defense, but they wouldn't take away guns from the American populace. Republican Representative, Edwin Arthur Hall, made reference to the Second Amendment in his proposal to Congress. The Second Amendment states simply: "A well regulated Militia, being necessary to the security of a free State, the right of the people to keep and bear Arms, shall not be infringed."

The Framers of the US Constitution and its Amendments were no dummies. They knew, first hand, of Europe's history of monarchs who would utilize standing armies and weapons control laws to dominate—and then exploit and murder— their own people. David Kopel convincingly argues that it was King George III's 1774 import ban on firearms and gunpowder imposed on the American Colonies, and the British General Thomas Gage's use of violence to confiscate firearms and gunpowder in 1774 and 1775 that precipitated the American Revolution.

We don't get the story of exactly how Golds came to power and subdued the Society, but we do know that all non-Golds in the Society lack weapons. So, at some point, the Golds must have confiscated or prevented the rest of Society from having weapons, and without them, all non-Golds lost the power to defend themselves against the power of the Golds.

"The Americans used their individual arms and their collective arms to fight against the confiscation of any arms," Kopel tells us, "Americans fought to provide themselves a government that would never perpetrate the abuses that had provoked the Revolution." Just as someone has the inalienable right to defend oneself from an aggressive person, so too, someone has the right to defend oneself from an aggressive government, organization, or social system.

The Second Amendment gives individuals a constitutional right to keep private arms, which is a reasonable deterrent against government attempts to institute a repressive political regime. This kind of *political freedom* to change or get rid of the governing body of a society is one of the hallmarks—if not *the* hallmark—of the American experience. The Second Amendment, then, can be viewed as protection for a civilian counterweight to the government's forces. It's the lack of this sort of political freedom that allows Golds to stay in charge. When such freedoms are granted the people gain the ability to change the government if they wish. Nowhere is this better illustrated than when the low-Colors are given access to weapons in *Morning Star*. They are immediately transformed from being oppressed slaves of the Society to being the means by which the government is toppled and the Society replaced.

Competent Colors and Helldivers

Who should get to bear arms in the Society of *Red Rising*? Competent adults should act as such, and should be treated as such, especially in societies where values like autonomy, respect, reasonability, responsibility, individualism, and freedom to do as one pleases (provided no one else is hurt in the process) are proclaimed as fundamental. Though the Society isn't there yet, it's where Darrow, Mustang, Sevro, Victra, and the others want it to be. So, all competent adults should be allowed weapons for protection.

Notice I say "competent adults." A competent adult who is also a gun rights advocate sees the need for firearms safety and training. When you hear of the tragic stories of kids killing others with guns, or killing themselves, and you investigate the facts of these circumstances, it's almost always the case that some irresponsible gun owner or instructor (!) is really to blame. In 2008, an eight-year-old boy was given an Uzi submachine gun to fire during a gun expo in Massachusetts and shot himself in the head, dislodging a section of his skull in the process. He died right there in his father's arms. All of this was caught on video, too, with family members having seen this first-hand. The President of the NRA at the time, numerous gun rights advocates, and almost every person on the planet thought that letting that kid fire an Uzi was a monumentally stupid idea.

These stories are tragic, but we can't eliminate all danger from our environments. People are killed accidentally in a myriad of ways: car accidents, fireworks, swimming, bicycling, school sports, even by mountain lions. And the lives lost in these accidents are a microscopic fraction of the lives saved by the thousand every day, when individuals use guns to protect themselves against murderous attacks. The government cannot and should not attempt to outlaw every instrument associated with accidental death. If we did the list would be pretty long and life would be less worth living— and our house gutters would never get cleaned without those deadly ladders.

Of course, there will always be those who abuse firearms while drunk or high, killing themselves or others, and there will always be those mentally incompetent folks who get a hold of firearms by "going through the system" who shouldn't have them. And we all know of the mass shootings that have taken place in the past fifty years in the US and all over the world. However, a blanket, draconian ban on all firearms is obviously not the answer.

As illustrated in *Red Rising*, and argued above, an unarmed citizenry is far more at risk of being harmed by individual aggressive assholes in that society or by aggressive assholes in control of the government, than an armed citizenry. In our society, when places like Washington, DC eased gun laws, murders went down from 186 in 2008, to 144 in 2009, 132 in 2010, 108 in 2011, and 88 in 2012. This pattern of "more guns, less crime" is repeated many times over in the statistics.

In *Red Rising*, the people's access to arms led to the toppling of an oppressive government and their systematic policies of slavery, rape, torture, and execution. It led to individuals having the right and ability to protect themselves, their families, and their fellow citizens from people bent on causing them pain and suffering, and it will hopefully lead to a stronger, more-stable, well-protected citizenry and society.

15
Death Begets Death

GREGORY L. BOCK AND JEFFREY L. BOCK

Darrow wants vengeance. His people have been enslaved by the Golds for centuries, and his father and wife were hanged. However, over the course of the trilogy, Darrow learns to control his anger and use it for more constructive ends. As Dancer, his Sons of Ares mentor, says, "I said I would give you justice. Vengeance is an empty thing, Darrow."

So, with Dancer's help, Darrow's anger is redirected toward the more positive and strategic goal of bringing about social justice by overthrowing the oppressive rule of the Golds. Yet the means to this end are morally troubling, for the Sons of Ares is a violent terrorist organization. And even though Darrow doesn't engage in terrorism himself (he almost does), his meteoric rise is built on a bloody military campaign that claims many innocent lives.

What if Darrow and his friends were to pursue a path of nonviolence instead? What if they were to love and forgive their enemies instead of slaughtering them?

Darrow's Anger

In the beginning, Darrow is filled with anger and seeks to avenge the death of his wife Eo by killing the ArchGovernor of Mars: "'I want to kill Augustus', I say, remembering the cold Golden face as it commanded my wife's death . . . 'He will not live while Eo lies dead'. I think of Magistrate Podginus and Ugly Dan. I will kill them too." His hate is directed at others as well. After Cassius stabs Darrow in the Institute and Darrow lies bleeding out in the cold mud, Darrow thinks to himself: "Rot in hell, Cassius. I was your friend. I might have killed your brother, but I had no choice. You did. You arrogant slag. I hate him. I hate Augustus. I see them hanging Eo together. They mock me. They laugh at me. I hate Antonia. I hate Fitchner. I hate Titus. I hate. I hate. I am burning and mad and sweating. I hate the Jackal. The Proctors. I hate. I hate myself for all I've done."

Darrow's emotions are understandable given all that he has suffered, and we'd probably feel the same if our loved ones were murdered and we lay bleeding in a ditch. Yet is such anger morally admirable? In Book IV of the *Republic*, Plato (427–347 B.C.E.) discusses the just man and identifies three parts of his soul: rational, spirited, and appetitive. He identifies anger with the spirited part of the soul and says that a just man is one in which the different parts of the soul work in harmony and are ruled by reason.

Plato asks, "Isn't it appropriate for the rational part to rule, since it is really wise and exercises foresight on behalf of the whole soul, and for the spirited part to obey it and be its ally?" According to Plato, anger is admirable when it's in accord with reason and only when the individual is under threat. He asks, "Wouldn't these two parts also do the finest job of guarding the whole soul and body against external enemies—reason by planning, spirit by fighting, following its leader, and carrying out the leader's decisions through its courage?" Darrow clearly has enemies, so his anger might be rational. However, Darrow often seems one step away from being consumed by his emotions.

In Book IV of *Nicomachean Ethics*, Aristotle (384–322 B.C.E.) calls the virtue concerned with anger "mildness," though he says the virtue doesn't actually have a name. A mild person gets angry "at the right things and toward the right people, and also in the right way, at the right time, and for the right length of time." The virtue of mildness avoids the extremes of having too little and too much anger. According to Aristotle, someone who doesn't get angry enough is "slavish," and someone who gets too angry is either irascible or bitter. Darrow definitely isn't slavish, and he's not completely bitter, but he doesn't have the virtue of mildness yet. At best, he's on his way to a temperate emotional state.

Blood Begets Blood

Dancer counsels Darrow to calm his anger and think about larger things: "When your wife died, she didn't just give you a vendetta. She gave you her dream. You're its keeper. Its maker. So don't be spitting anger and hate. You're not fighting against them, no matter what Harmony says. You're fighting for Eo's dream, for your family that is still alive, your people." Dancer's justice is a present and future-oriented justice that aims for equality and the end of oppression for those still living. Vengeance, on the other hand, is past-oriented. It focuses on the pain of the past and aims to get even. As Donald Trump says, "When somebody screws you, screw them back in spades."

Justice can also be past-oriented when it's about dispassionately giving people what they deserve. This is justice as retribution, also known as *lex talionis* or "an eye for an eye." It was made famous by Immanuel Kant (1724–1804) and is referred to several times by Darrow. For example, when he addresses the Jackal near the end of *Morning Star* he says, "Adrius, we are coming for you. We will break your ships. We will storm Mars . . . We will find you and *we will bring you to justice.*" Retribution is distinguished from vengeance in that retribution is supposed to be an objective, proportional meting out of what is deserved. Vengeance, on the other hand, is often disproportional and sometimes isn't satisfied until the wrongdoer has been utterly destroyed.

During the course of the Institute's training and tribal war games, Darrow learns the difference between vengeance and retributive justice when he punishes Titus au Ladros, his classmate and rival in House Mars. Titus rules his faction in House Mars with a heavy hand, raping, mutilating, and murdering those his group captures—until his castle is defeated by House Minerva. After Darrow's group wrests control of the castle back from Minerva and unites Mars, Darrow interrogates Titus and discovers the reason for his horrific behavior: Titus is another carved Red who infiltrated the Institute. However, Titus hasn't yet learned to let go of his anger and his thirst for vengeance. Darrow hasn't either, but he's not consumed by it to the extent that Titus is.

Darrow thinks to himself, "Titus is what Dancer did not want me to become. He is like Harmony. He is a creature of vengeance. A rebellion with Titus at the helm would fail in weeks." So, Darrow decides that Titus "is a mad dog, and must be put down," sentencing him to death. However, instead of carrying out the execution himself in a dispassionate way, he allows Cassius, who seeks to avenge the death of his brother, to carry out the sentence in a lopsided duel. Titus dies quickly:

> "That wasn't justice," he murmurs without looking me in the eyes. I failed the test. He's right. It wasn't justice. Justice is dispassionate; it is fair. I am the leader. I passed the sentence. I should have done it. Instead, I gave license to vengeance and vendetta. The cancer will not be cut away; I made it worse.

Titus and Cassius both represent the way of vengeance where "blood begets blood," and Darrow is learning that his own path must be different.

Yet the path of justice that Darrow ultimately takes is morally troubling as well because it involves the deaths of thousands of people, even innocents. For example, toward the end of the third story, Darrow and his team find themselves aligned with the forces of the Outer Rim planets. They use these forces to combat Roque and gain momentum as they try to work their way back to Mars. After Darrow and his team successfully board Roque's ship and fight their way to the bridge, they encounter the unrepentant Roque, who promptly ends his life in front of them.

Darrow is now faced with a choice. He has control of the ship and has won the day but knows that his alliance with the Outer Rim planets is a dangerous one. He says, "Romulus is an ally today, but I know he will threaten the core if the Rising succeeds." So, he turns the ship toward the massive docks at Ganymede. Under the guise of not being in control of the ship, allowing the Rim to think that this was the last desperate act of Roque and his forces, Darrow bombs the docks and kills thousands of innocents in the blink of an eye. "'There's still going to be thousands of Reds on there'. Holiday says quietly to me. 'Oranges, Blues . . . Grays'." The decision is brilliant military strategy—the Rim won't be able to threaten him for fifty years—but the cost of innocent lives, the very people Darrow is fighting for, is staggering. Is there a better way?

Loving Your Enemies

Martin Luther King, Jr. also fought for his people, but he didn't use violence. Instead, he advocated loving your enemies, which is what Jesus of Nazareth commanded. In the Sermon on the Mount, Jesus says, "You have heard that it was said, 'Love your neighbor and hate your enemy'. But I tell you: Love your enemies and pray for those who persecute you, that you may be sons of your Father in heaven" (Matthew 5:43–45).

According to Jesus, we are to love everybody, even those who do us wrong, because this is what God does. In Romans 5:8–10, the Apostle Paul says, "But God demonstrates his own love for us in this: While we were still sinners, Christ dies for us . . . For if, while we were God's enemies, we were reconciled to him through the death of his Son, how much more, having been reconciled, shall we be saved through his life!" Love is other-centered and self-giving. The one who loves gives herself for the sake of the other. In Greek, the word for this kind of love is *agapē*. In *Stride toward Freedom*, King says that *agapē*

is an entirely "neighbor-regarding concern for others," which dis-covers the neighbor in every man it meets. Therefore, *agape* makes no distinction between friend and enemy; it is directed toward both. If one loves an individual merely on account of his friendliness, he loves him for the sake of the benefits to be gained from the friendship, rather than for the friend's own sake. Consequently, the best way to assure oneself that love is disinterested is to have love for the enemy-neighbor from whom you can expect no good in return, but only hostility and persecution.

Forgiveness logically follows from the command to love our enemies. In Matthew 18:21–22, Peter asks Jesus how many times he ought to forgive a wrongdoer, and Jesus replies, "I tell you, not seven times, but seventy-seven times."

In *Forgiveness and Love*, Glen Pettigrove defines forgiveness as the forswearing of hostility (hostile reactive attitudes) and a commitment to the well-being of the offender. If we hold on to hostile feelings toward our enemies, we'll be unable to pursue their well-being. Forgiveness enhances their well-being because it sees their good, wills their good, and restores positive feelings in the relationship. In *Strength to Love* King writes, "He who is devoid of the power to forgive is devoid of the power of love." So, on the Christian account, forgiveness flows out of love. Let's call this *loving-forgiveness*.

Is loving-forgiveness of our enemies even possible? Certainly not if we see them as personifications of evil, for who can love someone who is thoroughly corrupt? If, on the other hand, we reflect on the humanity of our enemies and find something we have in common—something good—then perhaps it is possible. As King says in *Strength to Love*, "we must recognize that the evil deed of the enemy-neighbor, the thing that hurts, never quite expresses all that he is. An element of goodness may be found in our worst enemy."

This is what Darrow learns. In *Golden Son*, once he and Mustang arrive in Lykos, Darrow shares his secret past with her through the holoCube of his carving and soon finds himself staring down the barrel of her scorcher. He anxiously tries to justify himself and persuade her that he isn't a vengeful Red like Titus:

DARROW: You kept me from becoming a monster. Can't you see? . . . I was surrounded by the people who enslaved mine for hundreds of years. I thought all Golds cruel, selfish murderers. I would have caved to revenge. But then you came . . . and you showed me there was kindness in them. Roque, Sevro, Quinn, Pax, and the Howlers proved it too.

MUSTANG: Proved what exactly?

DARROW: That this isn't about my people against yours. You aren't Gold. We aren't Red. We're people, Mustang. Each of us can change. Each of us can be what we like . . . I see the love in you. I see the joy, the kindness, the impatience, the flaws. They're in me. They were in my wife. They're in all of us because we are human.

Darrow discovers goodness in the Golds, which enables him to be more compassionate. He is still angry, but perhaps he now has it in the right proportion as Aristotle recommends. Or as a Christian might say, he hates the sin but loves the sinner. He also discovers something else that he has in common—a flawed nature.

So, loving-forgiveness depends not only on recognizing the good in our enemies but also the flaws we share. It's our common humanity in which we find solidarity with others. As King points out in *Strength to Love*, "This simply means that there is some good in the worst of us and some evil in the best of us. When we discover this, we are less prone to hate our enemies."

Our default as victims of wrongdoing is to view wrongdoers as evil. We are righteous victims and the evildoer must be punished. This is an *us-versus-them* mentality. Instead, what's needed is an *us-together* mentality, one in which we remember that we have wronged others on occasion and have similarly needed forgiveness. In the Christian view, we find the ability to forgive in the recognition of a shared sinfulness, a recognition that we have all sinned and fallen short of God's glory (Romans 3:23). We forgive others because we have been forgiven by God (Ephesians 4:32, Colossians 3:13).

Darrow demonstrates forgiveness in *Golden Son* when he offers to forgive Tactus. Admittedly, this offer is initially just a tactical decision in an attempt to stop him from massacring Lorn's grandchildren, but then Darrow realizes he means what he says. He actually wants to forgive. He wants Tactus back. "Just leave the children alone, and all is forgiven," Darrow says. Tactus, in tears, apologizes and embraces Darrow, but Lorn is less forgiving and immediately stabs and kills Tactus in the name of "consequences."

Sevro also learns forgiveness. After the battle with Roque in *Morning Star*, the Obsidians and the Sons of Ares start a riot and try to execute the Gold prisoners. Darrow and Sevro try to reason with them, but to no avail. Sevro then claims Cassius as his own prisoner since Cassius killed his father. He hangs Cassius then hangs himself proclaiming that all murderers deserve to die. Sefi realizes the point Sevro is making, that forgiveness is more powerful than vengeance, and cuts them both down. Sevro's object lesson echoes Jesus's words: "He who is without sin, let him cast the first stone" (John 8:7).

Sevro then states his case for forgiving: "'Cassius au Bellona killed my father . . .' He stands over the man, swallowing before looking back up. 'But I forgive him. Why? Because he was protecting the world he knew, because he was afraid'." This also sounds like Jesus when he says on the cross, "Father, forgive them; for they know not what they do." In *Strength to Love,* King comments on Jesus' words: "We must recognize that Jesus was nailed to the cross not simply by sin but also by blindness. The men who cried, 'Crucify him', were not bad men but rather blind men." Like Cassius, they did not fully understand what they were doing.

Mustang forgives in a small but significant way at the end of the trilogy. She's been crowned Sovereign, and it looks like justice has finally caught up with her cruel brother, Adrius (the Jackal). As he hangs from the gallows, it looks as if his death will be slow and painful because there is little gravity on Luna. The tradition on Mars is to let loved ones pull on prisoners' legs to bring about a quick, merciful death, but it appears that he has no one to do this for him. Then his sister, in a remarkable act of compassion, comes forward to pull his legs, showing him, as the author says, "he was loved, even at the end."

Loving-Forgiveness and Nonviolence

So, our Rising heroes are forgiving, but there's a stark difference between the strategies of Darrow au Andromedus and Martin Luther King, Jr. For one, King didn't kill anyone; he engaged in nonviolent resistance. In *Stride toward Freedom*, King says, "Hate begets hate; violence begets violence . . . We must meet the forces of hate with the power of love." Darrow speaks of love—justice in the name of love—but he uses the tools of violence against his enemies. Darrow's "love" is reserved primarily for the lower, oppressed classes, although as we've pointed out, Darrow apparently doesn't think this precludes dropping bombs on the very ones he's trying to love in the name of "the greater good."

Is violence a morally acceptable way to bring about justice? King would say no. He says in *Stride toward Freedom*, "Constructive ends can never give absolute moral justification to destructive means, because in the final analysis the end is preexistent in the mean." He gives two reasons for rejecting violence as a tool for justice: 1. it is impractical in the sense that violence only begets more violence; and 2. it is immoral in that it involves hating your enemy.

King connects violence and hate because he says it's inconsistent to both love someone and try to kill him. This seems correct. He also thinks that loving one's enemy means using persuasion, not coercion. In *The Trumpet of Conscience*, King says, "Be assured that we'll wear you down by our capacity to suffer, and one day we will win our freedom. We will not only win freedom for ourselves; we will so appeal to your heart and conscience that we will win you in the process, and our victory will be a double victory." According to this view, the forgiveness Darrow and his friends offer is outweighed by the sheer amount of death they are responsible for; moreover, resentment may give rise to another rebellion in the future (the next trilogy?).

Is violence compatible with forgiveness? Perhaps—if we separate the personal from the political domain and say that forgiveness is a personal obligation and leave killing (war, capital punishment, and so forth) to the authorities. Some Christians use Romans 13:4 to support this view: "For he [the governing authority] is God's servant to do you good. But if you do wrong, be afraid, for he does not bear the sword for nothing. He is God's servant, an agent of wrath to bring punishment on the wrongdoer." On this view, retributive justice is the responsibility of the state, and violence has its proper place in a good society. Nevertheless, it's unclear whether this passage should be interpreted as a justification of violence, for punishment can take many (nonviolent) forms. Also, King's concerns about the ends pre-existing in the means must be addressed. If we hope, like Darrow and Mustang, to create a just society, how is that possible if in its construction the tools we use are unjust (or unloving)?

Darrow and his friends successfully overthrow Octavia au Lune and bring freedom to much of the Society, but can they keep the peace? Darrow suggests they can't. At the end of *Morning Star* he says, "The war is not over. The sacrifices we made to take Luna will haunt our new world." Death begets death. The issues raised in *Red Rising* are relevant for us today, and there seems to be more angry people than ever in our society. Perhaps it's time to listen to what King was trying to tell us.

16
Can We All Get Along?

COURTLAND LEWIS

We will do the best we can.

—DARROW, *Morning Star*

Imagine watching a person brutally execute someone you love dearly. It's tough to imagine, but this is exactly what happens to Darrow at the beginning of Pierce Brown's *Red Rising* trilogy.

He must endure not only the death of his father and wife, but as is the custom, he must pull on his wife Eo's legs to ensure her neck is thoroughly broken. Could you break the neck of the one you love, for something as mundane as singing a song? Imagine living in an oppressive society where slavery, rape, and torture aren't only commonplace, but are endorsed by social practices and the law.

What I'm asking you to do is to put yourself in Darrow's shoes. Now that you've done it, imagine living alongside the people responsible for the evils you encounter on a daily basis. When you meet a stranger, you don't know if he killed your father, raped your sister, or committed some other terrible crime. How could you actively participate in a society surrounded by people who've done such terrible things to you, your loved ones, and your fellow citizens?

This is exactly what the people of *Red Rising* must do. As we reach the end of *Morning Star*, we get only a taste of the political and social turmoil about to be unleashed on the Society. We know what happens to several of the Golds, but what happens to millions of other Golds (and people of lower colors) that committed similar wrongs and atrocities? Do you throw them all in jail, execute them, or let them go free? Do you let lynch mobs avenge all wrongs? Who gets to decide who's innocent, what's an actual wrong vs. a perceived wrong, and what sort of punishment is appropriate? Do you let the perpetrators go free, allowing them to reintegrate into society as though nothing ever happened? These are all difficult and complex questions, and they aren't limited merely to the world of *Red Rising*.

Life is full of wrongdoing, and we've all been both victims and perpetrators at some point in our lives. We've lied to someone, cheated someone, said something mean, and we've had the same done to us. In fact, human existence is full of suffering, torture, mental and physical abuse, terror, and murder, often followed by anger, spite, revenge, and wars that result from all of the above. Somehow we keep living together without completely blowing ourselves up—thankfully, we don't have too many Jackals!

When such wrongdoings occur, we must determine what should happen. For some, it's a simple matter of punishment. However, when the wrongdoing occurs on the scale of a society, punishing every wrongdoer isn't feasible, since doing so would both cripple society and likely lead to even worse conditions. So, when societies are involved in wrongdoings, we must rely on transitional justice—justice that attempts to transition a society from one of wrongdoing to one of mutual, just cooperation.

Apartheid Rising

Pierce Brown's dystopic *Red Rising* Society might appear to some as a mere fanciful tale of fiction, but the themes of torture, terrorism, oppression, and genocide have many real-life parallels, both contemporary and historical.

One disturbingly similar historical example is Apartheid South Africa. Apartheid was a system of legalized segregation that oppressed non-whites in South Africa. It effectively limited their participation in political and social activities, and led to the criminalization of many activities of non-whites, especially political protests. Native Africans were forced to live in substandard housing, and if they engaged (or were even suspected of engaging) in any sort of political protest, they would be arrested, detained, commonly tortured, and in many cases, given lengthy prison sentences or murdered. Darrow's Mars, where singing a song can get you killed, doesn't sound so fanciful anymore, does it?

Singing a song might seem mundane, but when that song carries with it a message of overthrowing those in power, it's a dangerous political tool. In Apartheid South Africa, similar acts of defiance often led to torture and murder. Since you're familiar with *Red Rising*, I trust you can handle graphic violence, but be prepared. Julian Edelstein's *Truth and Lies: Stories from the Truth and Reconciliation Commission in South Africa* presents us with the following mother's account of witnessing her son shot and killed:

> I went flying out of this house. Now I am dazed. I ran, not thinking. My eyes are on the crowd that has gathered—Here is my son, my only child. It was just blood all over. My anguish was beyond anything I ever thought I could experience. They have finished him. I threw myself over him. I can feel the wetness of his blood—I felt his last breath leave him. He was my only child.

Such an example is not unique. Archbishop Desmond Tutu describes several instances of rape, torture, and killing that are equally disturbing. In the Eastern Cape, it was common for people to simply "vanish." In one case, the police drugged and abducted an innocent young man. They then tortured, killed, burned his body, and used the fire to have a barbecue.

Not enough? One of the more popular methods of torture and killing was the "necklace," which placed an empty tire filled with petrol around a person's neck, set it on fire, and allowed it to burn itself out. And even though officials claimed such actions were necessary to protect "innocent women and children," the ones they killed were innocent women and children. In the name of protecting people with a certain skin *color*, government forces systematically oppressed people with rape, torture, killing, separating families, and letting families starve.

The Golds of *Red Rising* used the same methods to oppress all other Colors. Reds are mining slaves, Pinks are sex slaves, Blues are . . . You get the picture. They're all slaves, and Golds will do anything (even to their own Color) to retain power—lie, cheat, steal, rape, torture, murder, and so on. With Darrow and Co.'s victory, how should the Golds be treated, both on a personal level and on a social or political level?

I Shall Avenge You, Eo!

One response is to seek revenge. Peter French offers one of the best philosophical accounts of revenge in his two books, *Cowboy Metaphysics* and *The Virtues of Vengeance*. French's main worry is that without vengeance, morality risks becoming mere words in the face of evil—sort of like telling Aja she's a bad person, as she kills your family and slices you in half. So, he develops an account of "virtuous vengeance" that gives morality "teeth," in order to justify violence against wrongdoers.

French uses the notion of a right to punish, grounded in John Locke's argument for the natural rights of life, liberty, and pursuit of property, to argue that revenge is morally just, as long as it "fits" the wrong committed. If the punishment is lesser or greater than what the wrongdoer deserves, then it's unjust—either too merciful or too harsh. Either way, the wrongdoer doesn't get what he deserves.

There are so many places to start, but let's begin with Eo. Eo sings "Persephone's Song," a forbidden song that the

Golds see as a threat to Society and, therefore, treason. We could debate whether Eo's execution for singing the song is too harsh, but regardless of our feelings about capital punishment, Eo's execution isn't an act of revenge. The laws are clear that certain actions carry a penalty of death, and Eo knowingly chooses her fate by singing the song. So, no matter how legally or morally unjust her execution is, a discussion of revenge doesn't apply.

On the other hand, Darrow's attempt to overthrow Gold Society inspired by Eo's execution is an act of revenge. With no legal recourse, Darrow chooses to act outside of the law in order to punish all of Gold society for the death of his wife. The question we must answer is: Is the destruction of Gold society a fitting punishment for the execution of one girl? The simplest answer to the question is "No," since the death of one young girl hardly seems to justify the suffering and death of many thousands.

What's more, virtuous vengeance must punish appropriately, which requires calm reason to *soberly judge* what's required for a particular transgression. One might get lucky with the right punishment, but a virtuous decision requires some sort of rational consideration. Making a free rational choice, based on determining what contributes to flourishing is what makes an action virtuous. Darrow is rational from time to time, but his avenging Eo's death is anything but calm and rational.

A savvy reader will note that Darrow's vengeance is fueled by more than just Eo's death. Though Eo is surely the first and most important motivation, throughout the stories, his desire to punish Gold Society becomes much more complicated. He wants to punish Golds for all the harms, wrongs, and evils of the Society. So, maybe destroying Gold society for its systematic oppression is the calm and rational option.

The problem with justifying Darrow's vengeance on Gold society due to their oppression is two-fold. First, it ignores and covers up his desire to avenge Eo's death. Second, the people in charge of Gold Society aren't the ones who created the Society. Should they be punished for something they didn't cause? For instance, think of all of the kids Darrow kills at the Institute. Did Julian deserve to be punished for what his ancestors did? Darrow might claim self-defense, but as I argued in Chapter 7 of this volume, he could've chosen differently. He could have said, "I refuse to punish this innocent young boy for the death of Eo and the oppression of the Society," but he didn't. Julian, then, became a means to his end of revenge.

I don't mean to be too hard on Darrow, for he struggles with such issues as the story progresses. It's also never clear that he comes to terms with the death and destruction he must cause in order to bring Gold Society to ruin. I'll suggest an answer below, but instead of crafting an elaborate argument for or against Darrow's revenge, I'll leave it to the reader to decide. Like all good philosophy, you learn more by coming to your own well-reasoned conclusion than you do by accepting the answer someone else gives you.

I Shall Forgive You, Nero!

A second way to engage the aftermath of the Reaper's Rising is to seek forgiveness. To see how and why we might seek forgiveness, Jessica Wolfendale argues that we must first reject the notion of an unforgivable wrong, no matter how devastatingly evil, because once we say someone is unworthy of forgiveness, we become like the wrongdoer.

To view wrongdoers as *not* worthy of any sort of engagement, reconciliation, or forgiveness is to adopt aspects of the wrongdoer's moral outlook. In other words, by viewing someone as unforgiveable, you view them as being of less moral worth than others who deserve forgiveness, which means you've taken on the same devaluing moral outlook that the wrongdoer had when he wronged you. As a result, you communicate the same devaluing moral message, and you become willing to commit your own evildoing.

Darrow regularly justifies his acts of violence against Golds by noting their evilness. He demeans them for their lack of an afterlife, their cunningness, and willingness to prosper off of the slave-labor of others. Nevertheless, he takes on the same attributes in order to achieve his goals. He becomes what he despises, in order to destroy what he despises. He becomes his own enemy, and if it weren't for some really strong and patient friends, he might have become as deadly as the Jackal, ruthless as Aja, and oppressive as the Sovereign. These Gold (and other "Colored") friends, however, force him to change his outlook.

In order to avoid embracing our wrongdoer's moral outlooks, Wolfendale maintains that we should reject the notion that they're irredeemable and embrace an attitude of forgiveness. Forgiveness is too complex a concept to tackle in this chapter, but stated simply, it's usually seen as a disposition to let go of feelings of anger and resentment, and to seek some form of either neutral or affirmative reconciliation. Since we're most interested here in how the Society of *Red Rising* recovers from the devastation of the Rising, I'm going to focus on reconciliation. If you're interested in forgiveness, there are many wonderful books by Charles Griswold (*Forgiveness*), Margaret Holmgren (*Forgiveness and Retribution*), Kathryn Norlock (*Forgiveness form a Feminist Perspective*), and myself (*The Philosophy of Forgiveness*) that you should look into.

What Is Our Best?

As quoted at the beginning of this chapter, when faced with the daunting task of bringing wrongdoers to justice, while at the same time maintaining a stable society, Darrow makes the depressing statement, "We will do our best." Perhaps, due to the complex social and political structure of *Red Rising*, this is all we can hope for, but let's see if we can give a more hopeful response.

When faced with the same difficult problem of how to keep society together after the atrocities mentioned above, South Africa created a Truth and Reconciliation Commission. The Truth and Reconciliation Commission was designed to foster reconciliation throughout society, and as described by Martha Minow in *The Philosophy of Forgiveness*, had the power of granting amnesty, denying amnesty, cataloguing stories from perpetrators and victims, and proposing methods of reparations for victims. The Truth and Reconciliation Commission's goals were to discover facts, promote personal and societal healing through truth-telling, and repair injustices through reparations. The creators of the Truth and Reconciliation Commission hoped that forgiveness would eventually be achieved, but its main goal was to reconcile society, as a way of promoting the forgiving-attitude suggested by Wolfendale.

The Truth and Reconciliation Commission began by accepting applications both from wrongdoers and victims. The former had to apply in person and fully disclose all facts or misdeeds that could be fairly characterized as having a political objective. The Truth and Reconciliation Commission would then review and make decisions, based on other accounts, about the fullness and truth of a perpetrator's confession. After careful consideration, the Commission would decide whether or not the perpetrator's actions deserved amnesty or whether the perpetrator should stand trial for his or her actions.

Perpetrators who confessed had a greater chance of receiving amnesty, but amnesty was never guaranteed. Amnesty was conditional on what occurred and in what degree it occurred. Harsher crimes, or attempts to hinder an investigation could lead to litigation. The stories and accounts of perpetrators were then made public, so victims could know and understand what actually happened to themselves and/or loved ones. One of the main purposes of the Commission was to create a database of true accounts that would give victims the ability to know what happened to their missing loved ones. What is more, the Commission recommend reparations for victims, which came in the form of the knowledge of what happened, symbolic gestures of erecting monuments and naming ceremonies, and even some minor monetary settlements.

Did the Truth and Reconciliation Commission work? It's too early to tell, but here are some examples of hope and reconciliation. The most famous and compelling example is Nelson Mandela, who spent twenty-seven years in prison for trying to end the racist policies of Apartheid. For most of these years, he performed hard-labor in a lime quarry. Upon his release, instead of seeking vengeance and promoting violence, he became president of South Africa, where he promoted and achieved reconciliation throughout the country and the world.

Dullah Omar, who was targeted for death under Apartheid, played a pivotal role in creating the Truth and Reconciliation Commission, because he wanted to see all people given the right to seek amnesty, even the ones who poisoned him. Beth Savage, a woman who grew up in a home that supported anti-Apartheid policies and equal rights for all, was injured in an attack so that she was unable to care, bathe, clothe, or feed herself. At the Commission, when describing her experiences, she said:

> All in all, what I must say is, through the trauma of it all, I honestly feel richer. I think it's been a really enriching experience for me and a growing curve, and I think it's given me the ability to relate to other people who may be going through trauma.

And in regards to her perpetrator's seeking amnesty, she said this was not important to her, but

> what I would really, really like is, I would like to meet that man that threw that grenade in an attitude of forgiveness and hope that he could forgive me too for whatever reason.

Beth Savage's responses seem unimaginable, not because they're filled with hatred, but because they're filled with reconciliation and forgiveness. All of these examples show what is possible after events similar to those seen in *Red Rising*. Could the Society of *Red Rising* institute a Truth and Reconciliation Commission that might reconcile society and set it on a healthy path?

The Hope for a Future Mars

The first step to taking responsibility and seeking reconciliation is to admit your guilt and repent. Once you carry out your obligation to repent, further obligations typically follow. In some cases, simply saying "I did it, I am sorry, and I will not do it again" is enough, but in other cases, especially the ones discussed above involving heinous wrongdoing, this communication of repentance is only the starting point.

Take, for example, a wrongdoer's responsibility in South Africa's Truth and Reconciliation Commission. Wrongdoers had to fill out applications that fully disclosed all facts and misdeeds relevant to Apartheid. Filling out this application made them vulnerable, and if the confession was neither truthful nor complete, wrongdoers were seen as unrepentant and were prosecuted. After going through the application process, the stories and accounts of perpetrators were made public, so victims and society could know and understand what actually happened to their loved ones. In some cases reparations were made, and in all cases, wrongdoers were allowed to return to society with the expectation that they not participate in such wrongdoings again and that they'd work towards a state of reconciliation.

So, Step One requires those who committed wrongdoings to come forward and confess their crimes. For *Red Rising*, all Colors must be honest about what they did, or didn't do, and make themselves vulnerable. It's this shared vulnerability that shows we're all capable of committing wrongs, which further shows that we're all in need of mercy, forgiveness, and reconciliation. Furthermore, all colors must be willing to accept punishment for their wrongs. Part of the power of admitting guilt and saying "I'm sorry" is that you're vulnerable to punishment. You take ownership of what you do, and you commit to never doing it again. Only by being vulnerable to punishment does mercy, amnesty, or forgiveness apply; and even though the new society of *Red Rising* might not choose to punish all guilty parties, making yourself vulnerable to the threat of punishment is morally important.

On a more practical level, victims and wrongdoers are going to have to talk. Adam Michnik was a dissident in communist Poland during the 1980s, and under the leadership of Woljciech Jaruzelski, he was harassed, censored, jailed, and psychologically tortured. Instead of seeking revenge, he developed a philosophy of political engagement based on *dignity*. After the fall of communism, instead of simply condemning Jaruzelski, he sat down and talked to him, noting that "it's impossible to gain a correct impression" of the person who wronged me without actually getting to know him.

Michnik's conversation with Jaruzelski illustrates two individuals engaged in trying to understand each other by uncovering the truth of the past and seeking reconciliation. This isn't an easy or fast approach, but it's the one that Mustang promotes throughout the *Red Rising* series, especially as the story develops. If Darrow and the survivors of the Reaper's Rising wish to have any hope for the future, they must learn to talk and understand one another.

Finally, the Society is going to have to remember correctly its past atrocities. Slavenka Drakulić tells a story of the social responsibility of Croatia in remembering its role in the Holocaust. On her first visit to Tel Aviv, Drakulić was continually questioned about her responsibility—as a Croatian—for the Holocaust. Croatia exterminated approximately 17,000 Jews, Serbs, gypsies, and Croat communists. Drakulić, however, was born after the Second World War, and was surprised by the continual questions regarding whether or not she felt any regret or guilt for Croatia's genocidal actions.

Her response was along the lines of: Sure, I hate that such events occurred, but I had nothing to do with them—I wasn't even born. However, the more time she spent in Tel Aviv around those who actually suffered in concentration camps, the more she came to realize that her response was unsatisfactory. After careful consideration, she realized:

> in front of the victims and their relatives, it was much easier to defend yourself from the past than from the present. As far as the past was concerned, I could offer my regrets, but it was much more

difficult to explain what the Croatian government and Croatian citizens were doing today to deal with that past.

Every Croatian citizen bears a responsibility for his silent support of this government's attitude toward the Holocaust, which at the time was comprised of fascists who honored their fascist ancestors by naming streets after those who participated in the Holocaust.

So, according to Drakulić, being Croatian tied her to Croatia's history—it partially defined her. The same is true for the Colors of Mars. Just because they weren't born, or they weren't responsible for the laws and the castes of the Society, they're still responsible for embracing and allowing themselves to be defined by the atrocities of the Society.

As Drakulić suggests, if we support a group that openly celebrates its past wrongdoings, we too celebrate those wrongdoings. We take on a level of responsibility for those past actions by promoting the ideology that allowed for past wrongdoings. Such an acceptance could, then, lead to future wrongdoings. If we identify with groups responsible for past wrongdoings, we must take responsibility for rejecting those past wrongs and the ideas that led to them. So, everyone in the post-Color society has a personal and social responsibility to reject the ideas and affiliations that led to the atrocities and genocide of their past. In the words of Drakulić, "A person cannot view history as a series of incomprehensible acts of a leader or a government. Eventually he must understand that it also depends upon what he himself says and does." If we don't speak out against wrongdoings, past or present, then we passively promote the wrongs committed under the auspices of those ideas.

Darrow, Mustang, and everyone else in their society have a hard, difficult, and painful road to travel, but let me suggest they take each step with Michnik's proposed "dignified engagement"—engagement with, but opposition against oppressive policies and regimes, to foster a healthy society. Let the following words from Michnik be the post-Color society's mission and goal:

Can We All Get Along?

The maturity of nations, societies, and individuals is measured in terms of the way in which they live with their own history and their own life story. . . . I think it of great significance—and in some ways I count it a victory for both of us—that today we are able to talk about all this [oppression, dissention, torture, murder] without hatred, without hostility, and with mutual respect while remaining true to our own past.

Guide to the World of *Red Rising*

COURTLAND LEWIS AND KEVIN McCAIN

Purpose

Why include this guide? Well, my goodman or goodwoman, it's simple really. If it's been a while since you've read the *Red Rising* trilogy, then this guide can help jog your memory about key points. If you haven't read *Red Rising*, this guide can help you better understand the chapters contained in this book.

But, seriously, if you haven't read the trilogy yet, what the slag are you waiting for?

Now that we're clear about the purpose of this guide let's get started, prime?

Where and When?

For the most part the setting for the story of *Red Rising* is quite familiar—it's our own solar system.

Although Earth is mentioned, it's Mars and the moon (Earth's moon) that are major foci of the story. Despite these familiar locales, many things are different from what we know because *Red Rising* takes place hundreds of years in our future. In this future, humankind has developed reliable means of traveling throughout the solar system in short periods of time. They've also developed means of terraforming inhospitable environments, such as Mars, into livable, and in many cases lush, places for humans to dwell.

While these bits of technology seem quite pleasant, not all of humankind's efforts have been so benign. In *Red Rising* humans have developed all sorts of new weapons for harming and killing one another. And, perhaps most disturbing of all, through years of selective breeding and genetic experiments they have generated very different types of people. Groups so different that some claim that it isn't clear that they're even the same species, and some (bloodydamn bastards like the Jackal) use these differences to argue that some of these groups have more rights and stronger claim to the goods of the solar system than others. This genetic and social engineering is the basis for the Society.

The Society

The Society is the government and social order that is in place throughout the solar system at the time of *Red Rising*. The central idea of the Society is that the different groups of people that have resulted from years of genetic, social, and sometimes surgical modifications are best suited for various tasks. These different groups are identified by Color.

Below is a table with a rough description of each of the Colors and their roles in the Society.

Two things are worth keeping in mind about the Colors. First, regardless of how the division into Colors originally got started (we're told that it was a necessary division of labor for surviving in the early days of terraforming), the Golds, who rule the Society, now keep this division of Colors along with their prescribed roles in place to ensure that the Golds continue to rule. Second, the table that follows will help give you a sense of the Colors that make up the Society. However, if you'd like a more precise understanding of the various Colors, there's an easy way to get it: read the bloodydamn *Red Rising* trilogy!

COLOR	ROLE IN THE SOCIETY
Gold	Rulers (think nobility from medieval times, or even better— nobles from the Roman republic/empire)
Silver	Businesspeople
White	Religious leaders ("leader" is used very generously here— perhaps a better description would be functionaries that purport to be religious leaders)
Copper	Administrators
Blue	Spaceship crew (pilots, navigators, etc.)
Yellow	Medics and scientists
Green	Tech developers
Violet	Artists
Orange	Mechanics
Gray	Police and soldiers
Brown	Servants (primarily "indoor" work)
Obsidian	Super-soldiers
Pink	Prostitutes (more accurately, sex-slaves)
Red	Manual laborers (lowest status of unskilled laborers at best, often simply slave laborers)

Brief Synopsis

WARNING: Here Be Spoilers!

Here's the essential story in very broad strokes. If you want more of the specific details (either because you need a refresher or because you haven't read *Red Rising* yet), recall the advice above concerning learning more about the Colors: read (or reread) the bloodydamn *Red Rising* trilogy!

The protagonist of *Red Rising* is Darrow, a Red miner from Mars. Darrow is (mostly) content with his existence as a Helldiver in the mining colony of Lykos. When we first meet him he doesn't know about the true nature of the Society or his role in it. He, along with his wife, Eo, gets into some trouble at the time that the Archgovernor of Mars, Nero au Augustus, happens to be visiting the mine. Eo, more of a visionary at this point than Darrow, seizes the opportunity to speak out against the Society in the only way she knows how—by singing a forbidden song. Augustus promptly has her executed for singing this song and then leaves the mine. This starts Darrow off on a path that leads to the Society (at least at the core of the solar system) being brought low.

Darrow ends up working for the Sons of Ares, a group bent on bringing down the Society. The Sons have Darrow Carved so that he can pass for a Gold—maybe he even becomes a Gold? That's a question for philosophers—such as those who wrote the chapters in this book—and for you the reader to decide.

After becoming a Gold, Darrow infiltrates Society eventually becoming the heir of the same bloodydamn Augustus who had his wife executed. Through many struggles Darrow eventually kills the Sovereign of the Society and gives the solar system (at least the core—the planets nearest the sun are still loyal to the Society and those in the outer reaches of the universe are still under the control of a regime that is similar to the Society) a chance for a new way of life.

It's really quite a tale. If you haven't already, you should read it (and watch the movies when they come out too!)

Bibliographic Institute

Aquinas, St. Thomas. 2014. *Summa Theologica*. Translated by the Fathers of the English Dominican Province. New York: Catholic Way.

Aristotle. 1941. *The Basic Works of Aristotle*. Edited by Richard McKeon. New York: Random House.

Arthur, John, and William H. Shaw, eds. 2010. *Readings in the Philosophy of Law*. Upper Saddle River: Prentice Hall.

Badiou, Alain. 2012. *In Praise of Love*. Translated by Peter Bush. New York: The New Press.

Barton, Charles K.B. 1999. *Getting Even: Revenge as a Form of Justice*. Chicago: Open Court.

Bix, Brian. 2010. Traditional Natural Law Theory. In Arthur and Shaw 2010.

Brown, Pierce. 2014. *Red Rising*. New York: Del Rey.

———. 2015. *Golden Son*. New York: Del Rey.

———. 2016. *Morning Star*. New York: Del Rey.

Camus, Albert. 1991 [1942]. *The Myth of Sisyphus and Other Essays*. Translated by Justin O'Brien. New York: Vintage.

Chambers, Robert. 1994 [1844]. *The Vestiges of Creation: And Other Evolutionary Writings*. Chicago: University of Chicago Press.

Cooper, Jeff. 1997. *The Art of the Rifle*. Boulder: Paladin.

Darwin, Charles. 2009 [1859]. *On the Origin of Species*. New York: Penguin.

Descartes, René. 1993 [1641]. *Meditations on First Philosophy*. Translated by Donald A. Cress. Indianapolis: Hackett.

Drakulić, Slavenka. 1996. *Café Europa: Life after Communism*. New York: Norton.

Dworkin, Ronald. 2010. The Model of Rules. In Arthur and Shaw 2010.

Edelstein, Julian. 2002. *Truth and Lies: Stories from the Truth and Reconciliation Commission in South Africa*. Introduction by Michael Ignatieff and an Essay by Pumla Gobodo-Madikizela. New York: The New Press.

French, Peter A. 1997. *Cowboy Metaphysics: Ethics and Death in Westerns*. Lanham: Rowman and Littlefield.

———. 2001. *The Virtues of Vengeance*. Lawrence: University Press of Kansas.

Galliott, Jai, ed. 2015. *Commercial Space Exploration: Ethics, Policy, and Governance*. New York: Ashgate.

Gramsci, Antonio. 1971. *Selections from the Prison Notebooks*. Translated by Quentin Hoare and Geoffrey Nowell Smith. New York: International.

Griswold, Charles. 2007. *Forgiveness: A Philosophical Exploration*. Cambridge: Cambridge University Press.

Hart, H.L.A. 2010. Positivism and the Separation of Law and Morals. In Arthur and Shaw 2010.

Hobbes, Thomas. 1994 [1668]. *Leviathan*. Indianapolis: Hackett.

Holmgren, Margaret. 2012. *Forgiveness and Retribution: Responses to Wrongdoings*. Cambridge: Cambridge University Press.

Honore, Tony. 2010. The Dependence of Morality on Law. In Arthur and Shaw 2010.

Hume, David. 1993 [1748]. *An Enquiry Concerning Human Understanding*. Indianapolis: Hackett.

Hutcheson, Francis. 2008 [1725]. *An Inquiry into the Original of our Ideas of Beauty and Virtue*. Indianapolis: Liberty Fund.

Ketcham, Christopher. 2015. Forty Hectares and a Mu. In Galliott 2015.

King, Jr., Martin Luther. 1958. *Stride Toward Freedom: The Montgomery Story*. New York: Harper and Row.

———. 1963. *Strength to Love*. New York: Harper and Row.

———. 2011 [1967]. *The Trumpet of Conscience*. Boston: Beacon Press.

Kleck, Gary, and Marc Gertz. 1995. Armed Resistance to Crime: The Prevalence and Nature of Self-Defense with a Gun. *Journal of Criminal Law and Criminology* 86, pp. 150–187.

Kopel, David B. 2012. How the British Gun Control Program Precipitated the American Revolution. *Charleston Law Review* 6, pp. 286–331.

Lamarck, Jean-Baptiste. 2011 [1809]. *Philosophie Zoologique.* Cambridge: Cambridge University Press.

Lewis, Court. 2016. *Explorations of Forgiveness: Personal, Relational, and Religious.* Wilmington: Vernon.

Lott, John R., Jr. 2010 [1998]. *More Guns, Less Crime: Understanding Crime and Gun Control Laws.* Chicago: University of Chicago Press.

Merricks, Trenton. 1998. There Are No Criteria of Identity Over Time. *Noûs* 32, pp. 106–124.

Michnik, Adam. 1998. *Letters from Freedom: Post-Cold War Realities and Perspectives.* Berkeley: University of California Press.

Milton, John. 2004 [1667]. *Paradise Lost.* New York: Norton.

Minow, Martha. 1998. *Between Vengeance and Forgiveness: Facing History after Genocide and Mass Violence.* Boston: Beacon Press.

More, Thomas. 1965. *Utopia.* Edited by Edward Surtz, S.J. and J.H. Hexter. New Haven: Yale University Press.

Mulgan, Tim. 2006. *Future People: A Moderate Consequentialist Account of Our Obligations to Future Generations.* Oxford: Clarendon.

Nagel, Thomas. 2013. The Absurd. In Seachris 2013.

Neiman, Susan. 2002. *Evil in Modern Thought: An Alternative History of Philosophy.* Princeton: Princeton University Press. Its introduction is available at <www.susan-neiman.de/docs/b_preface.html>.

Norlock, Kathryn. 2009. *Forgiveness from a Feminist Perspective.* Lanham: Rowman and Littlefield.

Olson, Eric. 1997. *The Human Animal: Personal Identity Without Psychology.* Oxford: Oxford University Press.

Orwell, George. 1949. *Nineteen Eighty-Four.* London: Secker and Warburg.

Palmer, Donald. 1999. *Visions of Human Nature: An Introduction.* New York: McGraw-Hill.

Parfit, Derek. 1984. *Reasons and Persons.* Oxford: Clarendon.

Pettigrove, Glen. 2012. *Forgiveness and Love.* Oxford: Oxford University Press.

Plato. 1997. *Plato: Complete Works.* Edited by John M. Cooper. Indianapolis: Hackett.

Plutarch. 2001. *Plutarch's Lives Volume 1*. Edited by Arthur Hugh Clough. New York: Random House.

Rawls, John. 1971. *A Theory of Justice*. New York: Columbia University Press.

———. 1996. *Political Liberalism*. Including an additional Preface and Reply to Habermas. New York: Columbia University Press.

———. 2001. *Justice as Fairness: A Restatement*. Edited by Erin Kelly. Cambridge: Harvard University Press.

Rousseau, Jean-Jacques. 1987 [1755]. *Discourse on the Origin of Inequality*. Translated by Donald A. Cress. Indianapolis: Hackett.

———. 1987 [1755]. *Discourse on Political Economy*, translated by Donald A. Cress. Indianapolis: Hackett.

———. 1987 [1762]. *The Social Contract*. Translated by Donald A. Cress. Indianapolis: Hackett.

———. 1979 [1762]. *Émile, or On Education*. Translated by Allan Bloom. New York: Basic Books.

Sartre, Jean-Paul. 1993 [1943]. *Being and Nothingness*. Translated by Hazel E. Barnes. New York: Washington Square Press.

Seachris, Joshua W., ed. 2013. *Exploring the Meaning of Life: An Anthology and Guide*. Malden: Wiley-Blackwell.

Shoemaker, Sydney. 1984. Personal Identity: A Materialist's Account. In Shoemaker and Swinburne 1984.

Shoemaker, Sydney, and Richard Swinburne, eds. 1984. *Personal Identity*. Oxford: Blackwell.

Slote, Michael, 2001. *Morals from Motives,* New York: Oxford University Press.

Taylor, Richard. 2000. *Good and Evil*. Amherst: Prometheus.

Thomson, Garrett. 2013. Introduction. In Seachris 2013.

Tutu, Desmond Mpilo. 1999. *No Future Without Forgiveness*. New York: Doubleday.

Voltaire, François-Marie Arouet. 1759. *Candide, or Optimism*. Among the variety of available translations, see William Fleming's modernized version of Tobias Smollett's early translation, available at <oll.libertyfund.org/titles/voltaire-the-works-of-voltaire-vol-i-candide>.

Wolf, Susan. 2010. *Meaning in Life and Why It Matters*. Princeton: Princeton University Press.

Wolfendale, Jessica. 2005. The Hardened Heart: The Moral
   Dangers of Not Forgiving. *Journal of Social Philosophy* 36.
Žižek, Slavoj. 2016. Slavoj Žižek: Is Hegel Dead—Or Are We Dead
   in the Eyes of Hegel? A Hegelian View of the Present Age.
   <www.youtube.com/watch?v=rHP1OwivAL0>, timestamp
   1:17:00.

Howlers, Helldivers, and Peerless Scarred

ROBERT ARP, PhD, is a researcher doing work for the US Army with interests in philosophy and pop culture. See robertarp.com. In life, he's been Gold and he's been Red—all things equal, being Red still sucks worse.

GREGORY L. BOCK, PhD, is Senior Lecturer in Philosophy and Religion at the University of Texas at Tyler. His research areas include ethics and the philosophy of religion, and he has co-authored several pop culture and philosophy chapters with his brother Jeff, including chapters in *The Devil and Philosophy: the Nature of His Game* and *Divergent and Philosophy: the Factions of Life*. After participating in his first Iron Rain, someone heard him say, "I'm too old for this!"

JEFFREY L. BOCK has an MA in History and is currently working on becoming a teacher in East Texas. During his Institute training, he too crawled into a dead horse, but promptly fell asleep and missed most of the action.

DEVON BRICKHOUSE-BRYSON is a Gold (a reformer, to be sure, goodman!) who grew up on Luna, but prefers the country estates of Mars. He is currently on Earth studying as a PhD candidate in philosophy at the University of Tennessee, Knoxville. His interests include political philosophy and aesthetics, and he is writing his dissertation on aesthetic criteria of theory selection. He and his wife, who is also a philosopher, enjoy the opera on Luna and cruising in the Rim.

DARCI DOLL was born in a time and place where it was assumed your potential for excellence was determined by where you were born and the class that you were born into. Upon being introduced to philosophy she learned that the conditions of your birth, the station, sex, or color you're born to does not dictate what you're capable of. She has since spent her time helping break the chains of ignorance and social injustice by finding examples of philosophy in pop culture and by teaching philosophy at Delta College.

RANDALL M. JENSEN is Professor of Philosophy at Northwestern College in Orange City, Iowa. His philosophical interests include ethics, ancient Greek philosophy, and philosophy of religion. He has contributed chapters to many books like this one, including *Battlestar Galactica and Philosophy*, *Batman and Philosophy*, *Superman and Philosophy*, and *Ender's Game and Philosophy*. His favorite class to teach is Philosophy and Science Fiction. He's currently wondering what best practices he can borrow from the pedagogical experts at the Institute of Mars.

TIM JONES is a bit confused about what Color place he'd end up occupying in the Golds' Hierarchy. As a teacher of Literature at the University of East Anglia in Norwich and a frequent contributor to this series, he'd probably be a Violet. As an elected councilman for Norwich City Council, he'd perhaps be a Copper. Mix them together and you get a sort of muddy Brown, so he'd probably go with that if it didn't point uncomfortably to the truth of both of those roles making him nothing more than an aggrandized sort of servant.

JOHN V. KARAVITIS, CPA, MBA, was pleased to see his family's motto used in the *Red Rising* trilogy: "Rise so high, in mud you lie." To John, this motto is truly divine, and, when applied to his literary critics, quite the comedy. A daunting allegory, if you will. Yes, indeed.

CHRISTOPHER KETCHAM, PhD, earned his doctorate at the University of Texas at Austin. He teaches business and ethics for the University of Houston downtown. His research interests are risk management, applied ethics including that of space exploration, social justice, and East-West comparative philosophy. I ask you to consider the future and offer your opinion: will our own song of Mars be a lament, a eulogy, or a joyful hymn?

COURTLAND LEWIS, PhD, is Program Coordinator and Assistant Professor of Philosophy and Religious Studies at Owensboro Community and Technical College. He is the Series Editor of Vernon Press's series on the Philosophy of Forgiveness, co-editor of *Doctor Who and Philosophy* and *More Doctor Who and Philosophy*, and editor of both *Futurama and Philosophy* and *Divergent and Philosophy*. Courtland's Color is Tie-dye, an experimental reject ignored by other Colors because of his peaceful philosophical ways and love of science fiction.

KEVIN MCCAIN was born and raised a bloodydamn Red. However, he has done his best to infiltrate Gold Society and is patiently waiting for the Rising to begin. In the meantime he enjoys teaching philosophy and researching at the University of Alabama at Birmingham.

TRIP MCCROSSIN teaches in the Philosophy Department at Rutgers University, where he works on, among other things, the nature, history, and legacy of the Enlightenment. There's some disagreement, it seems, about the collaborative nature of his classes. "How do they get anything done?", some object. "They don't care about efficiency," others say. "They care about agreement. Watch."

BRENDAN SHEA, PhD, is a Philosophy Instructor at Rochester Community and Technical College, and a Resident Fellow at the Minnesota Center for Philosophy of Science. He's also currently serving as a member of the Institutional Biosafety Committee at the Mayo Clinic. His teaching and research focus mainly on issues within the philosophy of science and applied ethics. He also enjoys thinking about the connections between science fiction and philosophy, and has published book chapters exploring the philosophy of *Alice in Wonderland, Ender's Game, Jurassic Park,* and other works. Brendan has a great deal of fun teaching and writing about philosophy, and is eternally grateful that his students are nothing like the Gold teenagers of the Institute.

Index

Index